Every Man a D

MW01294911

Who is called to ordination as a
Roman Catholic deacon

Deacon Rex H. Pilger Jr PhD

Nihil Obstat: Deacon Owen F. Cummings, PhD, Censor Librorum

Imprimatur: +Most Reverend Samuel J. Aquila, STL, Archbishop of Denver, January 24, 2014

Contents

About the Author

Deacon Rex H. Pilger, Jr., and his wife Rita live in Arvada, a suburb of Denver, Colorado, USA. Rex and Rita celebrated their fortieth wedding anniversary in 2013. They are parents of five grown children and eight grandchildren (as of the date of this writing, August, 2014).

Deacon Rex was ordained to the permanent diaconate in 1988 and has served in five parishes in three dioceses. His ministry has included marriage and Baptism preparation, the homily at Mass, and lay ministry training. For ten years, he also was involved in formation of men seeking their deacon ordination, especially liturgy and preaching, marriage and baptism preparation, and the vocation of deacon.

Rex is a geoscientist by training and taught university geophysics and plate tectonics for thirteen years. He has published numerous articles and a monograph on plate tectonics and petroleum-related geology; many of the articles are accessible through his website: www. pilger. us.

Rex is grateful to so many pastors and deacons with whom he has served and from whom he has learned so much, and the bishops under whom he has served for their leadership, inspiration, and encouragement. Three deacons need to be acknowledged: Alfonzo Sandoval, John Smith, and Joe Donohoe, who each in his own way inspired and/or assisted with this project. He also thanks niece Jessica Comeau for her careful proofing of the manuscript. Married authors almost always acknowledge the support of their spouses as a particular task, such as a book, has taken the author away for uncounted days. Yet, my Rita's gift to this deacon-husband goes beyond the virtues of patience, intercession, and support, for the light of faith that she shares with others, especially a deacon-husband, is beyond description. Thanks, love-of-my-life, for all you have given me, our children and our grandchildren, in and through our Lord Jesus. Marriage has been a rocky adventure which we have shared every day along the way, good times and bad; so it is my prayer, indeed our prayer, that the sacramentality of our marriage brings others closer to our Lord.

Rex dedicates this work to grandchildren Jeb, Maddie, Abbi, Mackayla, Morgan, Lindsey, Andy, and Maisie, and those yet to come, and offers it to the greater glory of our Lord Jesus Christ, who came not to be served but to serve.

Deacon Rex can be contacted via email: rexpilger@yahoo. com.

Abbreviations

AA – Apostolicam Actuositatem, Vatican Council II – On the Apostolate of the Laity, 1965

AG – Ad Gentes, Vatican Council II – On the Mission Activity of the Church, 1965

BN – Basic Norms for the Formation of Permanent Deacons, Congregation for Catholic Education, 1998

CARA – Center for Applied Research in the Apostolate, Georgetown University

CCE – Catechismus Catholicae Ecclesiae – Catechism of the Catholic Church, 1993, 1997

CD – Christus Dominus – Vatican Council II, Concerning the Pastoral Office of Bishops in the Church, 1965

CIC – Codex Iuris Canonici – Code of Canon Law, 1983

DML – Directory for the Ministry and Life of Permanent Deacons, USCCB, 2005

DV – Dei Verbum, Vatican Council II – Dogmatic Constitution on Divine Revelation, 1965

FDC – From the Diakonia of Christ to the Diakonia of the Apostles, International Theological Commission, 2002

IGMR – Institutio Generalis Missalis Romani – General Instruction of the Roman Missal (Latin-2008; English-2010) (The English-literate population may know this by "GIRM")

GS – Gaudium et spes, Vatican Council II – Pastoral Constitution on the Church in the Modern World, 1965

IC – Interior Castle by St. Teresa of Avila

LG – Lumen Gentium, Vatican Council II – Dogmatic Constitution on the Church, 1964

PRR – Pontificalis Romani recognitio – Apostolic Constitution Approving New Rites of Ordination of Deacons, Priests, and Bishops, 1968

NABRE – Revised New American Bible, 2011

RS – Redemptionis Sacramentum, 2004

SC – Sacrosanctum Concilium, Vatican Council II – Constitution on the Sacred Liturgy, 1963

SDO – Motu Proprio, Sacrum Diaconatus Ordinem – Norms for Restoring the Permanent Diaconate, Paul VI, 1967

USCCB – United States Conference of Catholic Bishops

Introduction

Forty years and counting... First person memories of the Second Vatican Council are fading into the past, but its effects persist, in its sixteen documents and in specific directives they provided the Roman Catholic Church. But, were the changes introduced by the Council fruitful, and, if so, is the Council still bearing fruit? In the Western world, religious and priestly vocations have fallen off; in the developing world priestly vocations are on the rise, but, with the exception of orders such as the Blessed Teresa of Calcutta's Missionaries of Charity, the Dominican Sisters of Nashville and Ann Arbor, and similar orders, religious vocations continue to languish. It is not at all clear that these negative trends are a consequence of the Council. Rather, perhaps the most destructive, concurrent development to the Council was the arrival of the "birth control pill," and the consequent "sexual revolution" of the Sixties. In the West, especially, self-fulfillment became the rationale for rampant promiscuity, facilitated by the pill, slipping into a destructive mix of "no-fault" divorce, neglected children, and, most tragically, the aborted unborn. Family sizes are smaller, except in many Muslim nations, producing demographic crises in not only the West, but also Japan and even China, whose one-child-per-family is sowing the seeds of even greater cultural disaster to come.

In profound contrast to these trends is one of the apparent success stories that would not have occurred but for the Council – the restored Permanent Diaconate. Thousands of men, most of them married, have responded to the call of their bishops to become permanent deacons. There are nearly 40,000 deacons worldwide (including 17,000 in the United States alone), exercising a visible permanent ministry; previously the Order of the Diaconate, except for the short period between diaconal and priestly ordinations, had been hidden within the priest and bishop, for nearly fifteen hundred years. During the intervening time, diaconal ministry had been exercised charismatically, in part at least, first by monks and friars in the Middle Ages and then by emerging religious orders, typified by the Congregation of the Mission and Daughters of

Charity of St. Vincent de Paul. Of course, the priests of the Mission and similar orders were exercising their superseded diaconal ordination in conjunction with their priestly grace; in effect the visible ordinary ministry of the deacon was disguised by the chasuble. And the non-ordained religious were (and are) fulfilling the promises of their own baptism. Further, it has been even longer than fifteen hundred years since *married* deacons in the Latin Church legitimately exercised their ministry.

Are 40,000 deacons enough? With millions and millions of Catholics in the world, and even more who have not been evangelized and are, therefore, un-churched, why could and should there not be many more deacons to serve the baptized and evangelize the unbaptized? And, since married men can also receive ordination, why not every man, yes everyman, become a deacon (except for those celibates who go on to receive priestly orders)? Why not, indeed? Is there not a need? Consider the challenge posed by the numbers in Chart 1.1, as compiled by CARA (Center for Applied Research in the Apostolate).

Every ordained or vowed vocation, except the permanent diaconate, has shown a decline in the United States since 1980. Interestingly, the growth in the number of deacons is approximately equal to the decrease in number of priests since the mid-1970s. However, as emphasized below, the deacon is not a substitute for the priest, but, rather, a complementary ordained minister.

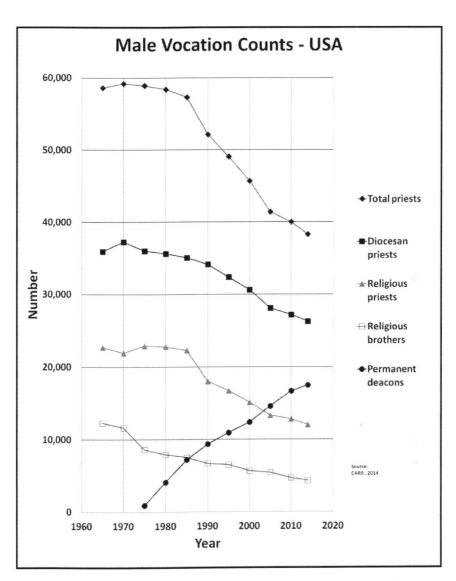

Chart 1.1 – Number of male Catholic vocations in the United States; data compiled by CARA as of 2014.

Global statistics demonstrate similar trends to the United States (Chart 1.2), but with a few exceptions. The decrease in vowed religious vocations is clear, but not as pronounced as the United States. Further, the number of diocesan priests is showing a slight increase in recent years.

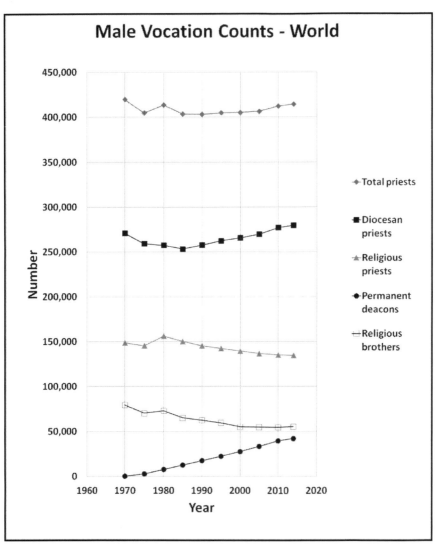

Chart 1.2 – Number of male Catholic vocations in the world; data compiled by CARA as of 2013.

The present number of deacons globally is significantly less than the number of priests, in contrast with the United States. By tradition, in Rome, seven deacons served the early Church and the Bishop, in imitation of the seven men called by the apostles to serve the Greek-speaking widows and orphans of the Jerusalem Church (Acts 6). What if there were seven deacons for every parish in the world?

Right now there are approximately six parishes for every deacon. In the United States, there is nearly one deacon, on average, per parish. (This is not to discount the serious need for more priests and religious, of course.)

This little book explores the ministry of the deacon for those Catholic men who may in fact be hearing a call to the diaconate, for the wives of such married men, for pastors who recognize the need for ordained *diakonia* in their own parish, and even for those men who are confident they have *not* been called (Are you sure, really sure?). It is also hoped that this work will also be of value to the faithful deacon, married or celibate, who is already fulfilling his ordination, and wants to more fully reflect on his ministry, as well as invite other men to consider their call.

The exploration may be a bit different from other books on the ministry. This contribution is unashamedly orthodox; that is, it accepts the Vatican Council II as *the* Council for our age. Vatican II accepted the validity of and is built upon the foundation of all preceding Ecumenical Councils. It is both a lens through which all of Tradition and Scripture is viewed, and is the source for all of the documents issued and formal actions undertaken since the Council by the Magisterium, the Holy See, and the Ordinaries of each diocese around the world. The history of the post-Conciliar documents themselves provides an interesting insight into the diaconate, particular insofar as peripheral controversies have arisen.

This is not the place to find a fond, nostalgic look at the pre-Conciliar Church or for visions of a future post-modern, egalitarian, gender-by-choice "worshipping community." On the other hand, there are theological implications of the restored ministry, in light of the peripheral controversies, which illuminate both past and, perhaps even future, while deepening understanding of not only the Sacrament of Orders, but some of the other Sacraments, as well. Some recent, less than formal, debates concerning the nature and exercise of the ministry of deacon particular with respect to marriage are unavoidable and, consequently, are confronted herein as well.

The current environment in which the Church finds itself – particularly its encounter with counter-Christian attitudes, perhaps even anti-rational forces – is the ambiance which the deacon cannot avoid. Thus this work must explore key theological implications of abortion, contraception, and nontraditional "marriage" to the ministry which the deacon is called. Often the married deacon is confronted with these issues in his own family life. Deacons, celibate and married, along with priests and bishops, must engage the controversies in marriage preparation catechesis and in proclamation of the Gospel of Life and the essential significance of the domestic Church, the family, within and outside of the Liturgy.

The author, along with many of his peers, is convinced that one of the principal ways the Spirit seeks to renew the Church of Vatican Council II – which continues to subsist in the Church of today-is through the restored diaconate, specifically including the majority of deacons who are married. The deacon is mentioned, understandably, in only a few of the Conciliar documents; in contrast, and unsurprisingly, bishops, priests, religious, and laity have documents devoted specifically to them; a close look at each of them, however, in light of *diakonia*, brings into sharper focus much of what the documents devoted to the ministry of service. The lack of a conciliar document devoted to the diaconate is understandable; the ministry had acquired and maintained its purely transitional status as the final step prior to the priesthood over the preceding centuries up until Paul VI restored the permanent diaconate. It is as if restoration of the diaconate to a "permanent" ministry would require much more specificity, reflection, and experience than a conciliar document could provide in a relatively short time. Subsequently, the nature of the ministry has acquired much more clarity, both in terms of what the Magisterium has taught and in the lived experience of 40,000 plus living deacons as well as those who have gone on to serve the Master in everlasting life.

The questions asked several paragraphs above cannot be answered without a basic understanding of what the ministry of the deacon *is*, who the deacon is, what the deacon *does*, and, perhaps most importantly, *why* there even is a diaconate. Flowing out of an understanding of the ministry are additional, more practical questions: What are the prerequisites for a man to be considered for the ministry? Are there factors that would prevent a man from entering formation for the ministry? What are the roles of the wife of married inquirers in preparation for entry into formation, during the formation itself, and after ordination?

The answers to such questions are based on Church law, rooted in Sacred Scripture (extending back to the Levitical ministry of the Old Testament) and Sacred Tradition, and expressed in our time in the Documents of Vatican Council II (1963-1965) and subsequent papal pronouncements, other official Vatican documents, and, especially the Code of Canon Law (1983) and the Catechism of the Catholic Church [*CCE*] (1997). Additionally, the conferences of bishops of individual countries, such as the United States Conference of Catholic Bishops (USCCB), formulate specific norms governing the ministry and formation, and each bishop who welcomes the ministry of the deacon in his diocese, promulgates particular laws that govern the ministry under his direction.

Ultimately it is the Holy Spirit who calls a man to Holy Orders, through the Church and the man's own sense of vocation. Joint discernment by the man, in concert with his wife (if married), pastor, spiritual director, and those responsible for diaconate formation, leads by a series of steps, towards or away from ordination. While a man or his wife or his pastor may have a strong sense of his call, discernment by the formation director and his team, nevertheless, is executed in concrete actions and ultimately subject to confirmation by the bishop in accord with Church law. Church law, built on a foundation of Natural and Divine Law, and relevant to the diaconate consists of Canon Law, norms promulgated by the Vatican, national bishop conferences, and the "particular" law of each diocese. As the purpose of Church law is to protect the rights of each member and the goods of the Church, both spiritual and temporal (material resources), part of the discernment process is to carefully and prayerfully fulfill each of its statutes.

One who may aspire to the ministry of the deacon is already, by necessity, a layman (or, for those male religious orders which have a permanent diaconate ministry, a lay brother). Focusing on laymen, exclusive of religious, such men will have been baptized and confirmed, are living a faithful Christian life, receive the Eucharist each Sunday and holy day, and the Sacrament of Reconciliation frequently. If married (validly, in the Church), each husband is faithful to his wife, passionately attached to her, and is a strong, gentle father to their children.

A man who wants to be considered for the diaconate must already be living out his baptismal promises. In calling for the restoration of the diaconate, the Fathers at Vatican Council II did not provide a comprehensive overview of the ministry of the deacon; in effect this was left to Paul VI, especially, and his successors. But, the Council did provide an elaborate discussion of the ministry of the laity in their Decree on the Apostolate of Lay People (*Apostolicam Actuositatem* [*AA*]). Since admission of a man to deacon formation presupposes he is an active faithful Catholic layman, it is appropriate to examine the apostolate of the laity itself as part of the investigation of the diaconate.

As one reads through the text of this book, repetition of certain texts will be apparent. Those which are duplicated are emphasized in different contexts so as to impress on that man who is serious about his ministerial vocation – lay or cleric – what the Church teaches relative to the diaconate.

What is a deacon? What does he do?

It is difficult to separate the "what" and "who" of a deacon from the "doing" of a deacon. In some sense, the function of the order is close to its identity.

Some years ago, a then diocesan director of the deacons observed and listened in on a reunion of newly ordained deacons. What they were talking about, he recounted, was what each one was doing. They were especially impressed with the number of baptisms being performed by one of their number in a parish with a large number of young Hispanic families: as many as twenty or thirty per month (or was it per week?)! What should be our perception of this observation? If these numbers of baptisms were cited as an answer to a question: "What has it been like to be a deacon these past few months?" then it's fair to be concerned, unless the answer that neo-deacon provided was a proxy for an answer like this: "It's been awesome. I've been gifted with the opportunity to welcome all these new children into the Church and observe the witness of the faith of their parents and godparents as the light of Christ is reflected on the faces of those little girls and boys. It's humbling and, at the same time, it's elevating; it strengthens my own faith and makes me so happy that Christ and His Church have called me to serve Him as an ordained minister."

Let's look at the "that" for which a deacon is ordained to do, perhaps illuminating who he has become by the laying-on-of-hands. *Lumen Gentium*[LG], the Dogmatic Constitution on the Church, of Vatican Council II, citing St. Ignatius of Antioch's Letter to the Romans, states (**emphasis** added):

> Bishops, therefore, with their helpers, the priests and **deacons**, have taken up the service of the community, presiding in place of God over the flock, whose shepherds they are, as teachers for doctrine, priests for sacred worship, and ministers for governing. (*LG* 20)

The priest and deacon are observed by St. Ignatius to be in close relationship to their bishop. They assist the bishop in his service of

9

the community, presiding over the flock (in the place of God, citing St. Ignatius) as shepherd, in the three-fold roles of teacher, priest, and governor. However, there are important distinctions among the three ministries. Further:

> Christ, whom the Father has sanctified and sent into the world, has through His apostles, made their successors, the bishops, partakers of His consecration and His mission. They have legitimately handed on to different individuals in the Church various degrees of participation in this ministry. Thus the divinely established ecclesiastical ministry is exercised on different levels by those who from antiquity have been called bishops, priests and **deacons**. (*LG*28),

Noting their antiquity, *LG* cites the Council of Trent in specifically recognizing the three levels of ministry. After an extended discussion of the ministry of the priest, *LG* makes this statement:

> At a lower level of the hierarchy are **deacons**, upon whom hands are imposed "not unto the priesthood, but unto a ministry of service." [footnote: *"ordinetur non ad sacerdotium, sed ad ministerium episcopi," Constitutiones Ecclesiac Aegyptiacae*].

> For strengthened by sacramental grace, in communion with the bishop and his group of priests they serve in the **diaconate of the liturgy, of the word, and of charity to the people of God.** It is the duty of the **deacon**, according as it shall have been assigned to him by competent authority,

> to administer baptism solemnly,

> to be custodian and dispenser of the Eucharist,

> to assist at and bless marriages in the name of the Church,

> to bring Viaticum to the dying,
> to read the Sacred Scripture to the faithful,

> to instruct and exhort the people,

> to preside over the worship and prayer of the faithful,

to administer sacramentals,

to officiate at funeral and burial services.

Dedicated to duties of charity and of administration, let **deacons** be mindful of the admonition of Blessed Polycarp: "Be merciful, diligent, walking according to the truth of the Lord, who became the servant of all."

Since these duties, so very necessary to the life of the Church, can be fulfilled only with difficulty in many regions in accordance with the discipline of the Latin Church as it exists today, the **diaconate** can in the future be restored as a proper and permanent rank of the hierarchy. It pertains to the competent territorial bodies of bishops, of one kind or another, with the approval of the Supreme Pontiff, to decide whether and where it is opportune for such **deacons** to be established for the care of souls. With the consent of the Roman Pontiff, this **diaconate** can, in the future, be conferred upon men of more mature age, even upon those living in the married state. It may also be conferred upon suitable young men, for whom the law of celibacy must remain intact. (*LG* 29)

Deacons are *not* priests, nor do they share in the ministerial priesthood, as we shall see in more detail below. Their ordination to a ministry of service provides strengthening via laying on of the hands of the bishop. The strengthening by this sacramental grace is to the ministry of the threefold service.

The *munera* (plural; singular is *munus*, meaning function, responsibility, duty...) of *Lumen Gentium* were instituted by Paul VI (in his *Motu Proprio, Sacrum Diaconatus Ordinem* [*SDO*]: General Norms for Restoring the Permanent Diaconate in the Latin Church), expressed in the revised ordination rite, and elaborated by the Code of Canon Law 1983. The *munera* of *Lumen Gentium*, together with their institution, expression, and elaboration according to the three subsequent documents, are provided in Table 1.

Table 1: *Munera* (functions and responsibilities) **of Deacons**			
Lumen Gentium	*SDO* of Paul VI	Ordination Rite	1983*CIC*
To administer baptism solemnly	To administer baptism solemnly and to supply the ceremonies which may have been omitted when conferring it on children or adults	It will also be his duty, at the bishop's discretion, to baptize. . .	Can. 861 §1. The ordinary minister of baptism is a bishop, a presbyter, or a deacon . . .
To be custodian and dispenser of the Eucharist. . .	To reserve the Eucharist and to distribute it to himself and to others ...	As a minister of the altar he will ... prepare the sacrifice, and give the Lord's body and blood to the community of believers	Can. 910 §1. The ordinary minister of holy communion is a bishop, presbyter, or deacon.
To assist at and bless marriages in the name of the Church. . .	In the absence of a priest, to assist at and to bless marriages in the name of the Church by delegation from the bishop or pastor observing the rest of the requirements which are in the [1919]*CIC*[8] with Canon 1098 remaining firm and where what is said in regard to the priest is also to be	[A]t the bishop's discretion, ... to assist at marriages and bless them. . .	Can. 1108 §1. Only those marriages are valid which are contracted before the local ordinary, pastor, or a priest or deacon delegated by either of them, who assist... Can. 1111 §1. As long as they hold office validly, the local ordinary and the pastor can delegate to priests and

	understood in regard to the deacon. . .		deacons the faculty, even a general one, of assisting at marriages within the limits of their territory.
To bring Viaticum to the dying. . .	To bring it as a Viaticum to the dying . . .	[A]t the bishop's discretion, ... to give viaticum to the dying. . .	Can. 921 §1. The Christian faithful who are in danger of death from any cause are to be nourished by holy communion in the form of Viaticum. Can. 922 Holy Viaticum for the sick is not to be delayed too long; those who have the care of souls are to be zealous and vigilant that the sick are nourished by Viaticum while fully conscious.
To read the Sacred Scripture to the faithful. . .	To read the sacred books of Scripture to the faithful ...	As a minister of the altar he will proclaim the Gospel	Can. 757 ... It is also for deacons to serve the people of God in the ministry of the word in communion with the bishop and his presbyterium.
To instruct and exhort the people	To instruct and exhort the people	[A]t the bishop's discretion, ... to bring God's word to believer and	Can. 764 . . . deacons possess the faculty of preaching

		unbeliever alike. . .	everywhere; this faculty is to be exercised with at least the presumed consent of the rector of the church, unless the competent ordinary has restricted or taken away the faculty or particular law requires express permission. Can. 767 §1. Among the forms of preaching, the homily, which is part of the liturgy itself and is reserved to a priest or deacon, is preeminent. . .
To preside over the worship and prayer of the faithful. . .	To preside at the worship and prayers of the people when a priest is not present. . .	[A]t the bishop's discretion, ... to preside over public prayer. . .	Can. 1009 §3. ... deacons are empowered to serve the People of God in the ministries of the liturgy, the word, and charity.
To administer sacramentals	To administer sacramentals. . .	. . .	Can. 1168 The minister of sacramentals is a cleric who has been provided with the requisite power.
To officiate at	To officiate at	[At] the bishop's	Can. 1009 §3. . . .

funeral and burial services.	funeral and burial services	discretion . . . to lead the rites of burial.	deacons are empowered to serve the People of God in the ministries of the liturgy, the word, and charity.
. . .	To assist the bishop and the priest during liturgical actions in all things which the rituals of the different orders assign to him...	. . .	Can. 835 §3. Deacons have a part in the celebration of divine worship according to the norm of the prescripts of the law.
. . .	To impart to the people benediction with the Blessed Sacrament with the sacred ciborium. . .	. . .	Can. 943 The minister of exposition of the Most Blessed Sacrament and of Eucharistic benediction is a priest or deacon. . .
. . .	To direct the liturgy of the word, particularly in the absence of a priest. . .	. . .	Can. 757 ... It is also for deacons to serve the people of God in the ministry of the word in communion with the bishop and his presbyterium.
. . .	To carry out, in the name of the hierarchy, the duties of charity and of administration as well as works of	[At} the bishop's discretion ... he will perform works of charity in the name of the bishop or the	Can. 1009 §3. . . . deacons are empowered to serve the People of God in the ministries of the liturgy, the word,

15

	social assistance.	pastor.	and charity.
. . .	To guide legitimately, in the name of the parish priest and of the bishop, remote Christian communities. . .	. . .	Can. 517 §2. If, because of a lack of priests, the diocesan bishop has decided that participation in the exercise of the pastoral care of a parish is to be entrusted to a deacon, . . . he is to appoint some priest who, provided with the powers and faculties of a pastor, is to direct the pastoral care.
. . .	To promote and sustain the apostolic activities of laymen.	. . .	Can. 1009 §3. . . . deacons are empowered to serve the People of God in the ministries of the liturgy, the word, and charity.
. . .	. . .	. . .	Can. 1169 §3. A deacon can impart only those blessings expressly permitted by law.

A deacon (or even priest) might think of each of these responsibilities as purely functional. However, each of them is assigned to and exercised by, under *ordinary* circumstances, the *ordained* only. The ordained minister's presence is in varying ways, essential; his personhood and the added, indelible character of the sacrament of ordination is somehow relevant.

> As in the case of Baptism and Confirmation this share in Christ's office is granted once for all. The sacrament of Holy Orders, like the other two, confers an *indelible spiritual character* and cannot be repeated or conferred temporarily. (*CCE*, 1582; *emphasis* added)

After the laying-on-of-hands, the bishop hands the Book of the Gospels to the ordinand, saying:

> Receive the Gospel of Christ whose herald you have become. Believe what you read, teach what you believe, and practice what you teach.

The deacon becomes a herald, not only by function, but by acquisition of a new, supernatural character which he will carry, along with baptism and confirmation, into eternity.

Further, notice that each of the deacon's *munera* is usually identified with the ministry of the priest. It is the priest who usually baptizes, preaches, leads in the distribution of Holy Communion, and so on. Yet, the individual person of the priest himself actually received the faculty to baptize, preach, and distribute Communion when he was ordained a deacon. In effect, these responsibilities not only continue but are enlarged upon the transitional deacon's ordination to the priesthood; he preaches more often, even daily, for example. And, of course, the priest receives the additional, essential power to confect the sacred species, hear confessions and give absolution, anoint the sick and the dying, and, under prescribed conditions, confirm the newly baptized catechumens and non-Catholics who are received into the Church. Nevertheless, when a priest exercises those faculties which he first received upon his diaconal ordination, one might see that the exercise is founded on and flows out of the ministerial *diakonia*. The ministry of deacon in the priest is hidden nominally beneath the chasuble, but emerges when he preaches, baptizes, proclaims the Gospel, distributes Holy Communion, and reaches out to the poor, widows, and orphans.

And, yes, his priestly ordination manifests itself when these aspects of ministry are exercised.

What is a deacon? What can he do?

In light of the functions that a deacon exercises, what can we say about the identity of this ordained minister? *LG* asserts:

> Christ, whom the Father has sanctified and sent into the world, (Jn. 10:36) has through His apostles, made their successors, the bishops, partakers of His consecration and His mission. (Cf. Gal. 4:19) They have legitimately handed on to different individuals in the Church various degrees of participation in this ministry. Thus the divinely established ecclesiastical ministry is exercised on different levels by those who from antiquity have been called bishops, priests and deacons. (*LG* 28)

The ministry of deacon is divinely established. It is important to emphasize, repeatedly, that deacons are not priests; neither do they share in the ministerial priesthood. Conversely, however, in order to be a priest, a man must have first been ordained a deacon.

> At a lower level of the hierarchy are deacons, upon whom hands are imposed "not unto the priesthood, but unto a ministry of service." (Jn. 21:17) For strengthened by sacramental grace, in communion with the bishop and his group of priests they serve in the diaconate of the liturgy, of the word, and of charity to the people of God. (*LG* 29)

The deacon receives a sacramental grace from ordination by the bishop, and this grace cannot be experienced and exercised separate from the highest level of the hierarchy.

> ... Now, in order to plant the Church and to make the Christian community grow, various ministries are needed, which are raised up by divine calling from the midst of the faithful congregation, and are to be carefully fostered and tended to by all. Among these are the offices of priests, of **deacons**, and of catechists, and Catholic action. Religious men and women likewise, by their prayers and by their active work, play an indispensable role in rooting and strengthening the Kingdom of Christ in souls, and in causing

it to be spread. (*Ad Gentes* [*AG*], Decree On the Missionary Activity of the Church,15)

The ministry of deacon is necessary. Even in the absence of the deacon, the Church's *diakonia* must still be exercised.

> Joyfully the Church gives thanks for the priceless gift of the priestly calling which God has granted to so many youths among those nations but recently converted to Christ. For the Church drives deeper roots in any given sector of the human family when the various faithful communities all have, from among their members, their own ministers of salvation in the order of bishops, priests, and **deacons**, serving their own brethren, so that the young churches gradually acquire a diocesan structure with their own clergy. ... Where episcopal conferences deem it opportune, the order of the **diaconate** should be restored as a permanent state of life according to the norms of the Constitution "*De Ecclesia*." For there are men who actually carry out the functions of the **deacon's** office, either preaching the word of God as catechists, or presiding over scattered Christian communities in the name of the pastor and the bishop, or practicing charity in social or relief work. It is only right to strengthen them by the imposition of hands which has come down from the Apostles, and to bind them more closely to the altar, that they may carry out their ministry more effectively because of the sacramental grace of the **diaconate**. (*AG* 16; "*De Ecclesia*," above, is *Lumen Gentium*).

Men ministering as catechists, parochial associates, and charity workers are manifestations of the Church's *diakonia*, which can be strengthened in them via ordination, thereby attaching each man more closely to the source and summit of the Church's life.

> In exercising their office of sanctifying, bishops should be mindful that they have been taken from among men and appointed their representative before God in order to offer gifts and sacrifices for sins. Bishops enjoy the fullness of the

sacrament of orders and both presbyters and **deacons** are dependent upon them in the exercise of their authority. For the presbyters are the prudent fellow workers of the episcopal order and are themselves consecrated as true priests of the New Testament, just as **deacons** are ordained for the ministry and serve the people of God in communion with the bishop and his presbytery. Therefore bishops are the principal dispensers of the mysteries of God, as well as being the governors, promoters, and guardians of the entire liturgical life in the church committed to them. (*Christus Dominus* [*CD*], Decree Concerning the Pastoral Office Bishops in the Church, 15)

The deacon has a special relationship of dependence on his bishop and share in communal ministry with his bishop and priests.

The three sacraments of Baptism, Confirmation, and Holy Orders confer, in addition to grace, a sacramental *character* or "seal" by which the Christian shares in Christ's priesthood and is made a member of the Church according to different states and functions. This configuration to Christ and to the Church, brought about by the Spirit, is indelible, it remains for ever in the Christian as a positive disposition for grace, a promise and guarantee of divine protection, and as a vocation to divine worship and to the service of the Church. Therefore these sacraments can never be repeated. (Catechism of the Catholic Church [*CCE*] 1121)

Paul VI, Apostolic Letter Given *Motu Proprio, SDO* – General Norms for Restoring the Permanent Diaconate in the Latin Church:

Although some functions of the deacons, especially in missionary countries, are in fact accustomed to be entrusted to lay men it is nevertheless "beneficial that those who perform a truly diaconal ministry be strengthened by the imposition of hands, a tradition going back to the Apostles, and be more closely joined to the altar so that they may more effectively carry out their ministry through the

21

sacramental grace of the diaconate." [AG] Certainly in this way the special nature of this order will be shown most clearly. It is not to be considered as a mere step towards the priesthood, but it is so adorned with its own indelible character and its own special grace so that those who are called to it "can permanently serve the mysteries of Christ and the Church." [SDO]

There are some who believe that one of the most significant changes introduced by Vatican Council II, and instituted by Paul VI, is the restoration of the permanent diaconate. It is further apparent that the full significance of the restoration is yet to be realized, as is similarly true of much else for which the Council called. Perhaps further fulfillment of Vatican II involves placement of the restored diaconate in context of the larger Conciliar themes. The universal call to holiness comes to mind, along with reformation of the sacred liturgy, and permission for its exercise in the vernacular. There is clarity in the practical and doctrinal theology of the episcopacy (bishopric) and presbyterate (priesthood), and definition of the ways in which the visible Church is to engage the rest of the world, especially through the apostolate of the laity.

Let's return to the restoration of the permanent diaconate by Pope Paul VI in 1967, as requested by the fathers at Vatican Council II. It has resulted, by 2012, in nearly 40,000 deacons active in twenty countries. (Statistics in this paragraph are taken from CARA.) This looks like an impressive number, especially in relation to largely declining numbers of priests and vowed religious in the West over the same period of time. However, if we consider the potential, say the number of global parishes (approximately 220,000) times the traditional number of deacons in ancient Rome, seven, we see a tremendous opportunity: 1,540,000 deacons. Or, imagine seven deacons serving with each priest: approximately 410,000 * 7 = 2,870,000! So, given about 1.18 billion Catholics, worldwide: that would mean one deacon for roughly 400 to 800 Catholics; my current home parish should have at least ten deacons (it has three) by this accounting.

Such back-of-the-envelope calculations neither demonstrate nor accomplish much of significance, however, because they beg critical questions: What is a deacon for? Do we need more deacons? And, then, if we need more, how many? Lastly, each deacon has his own gifts and talents, so which deacons should be assigned what ministries?

Numerous books and articles on the nature of the diaconate have emerged in the intervening years since Paul VI's 1967 *Motu Proprio*. Some are out-of-date at least in part, in that important new and illuminating documents have been issued by the Holy See in the last twenty years, especially the Catechism of the Catholic Church and combined Norms for Formation of and Directory for Permanent Deacons; further, clarifications of certain issues by the Holy See, including the Holy Father himself, have been made in the last few years. There is also the continuously deepening and enriching theology and philosophy provided by the Magisterium: the four post-Conciliar popes (yes, even including John Paul I, who led the Church for only 33 days), the teaching Congregations, and individual cardinals and bishops, on those topics which are so pertinent to the diaconate: marriage, chastity, celibacy, family, Christian anthropology. . .

This work examines the nature of the ministry, in light of recent clarifications which reemphasize the teachings of Vatican Council II and the consistent tradition of Holy Mother Church, especially manifested in Sacred Scripture.

The title of this work is an attempted and unashamed hook, if not a straw man. Of course, one might respond to "Every...man a deacon?" thusly: There are a lot of men who cannot be Roman Catholic deacons. (Ah, yes, the first, but critical, qualifier – RC! But, after all, it is present in the subtitle). There are those who lack the intellectual capacity, or those in invalid marriages, or those with demanding professions or ... the list of apparent exceptions goes on. Part of the thrust of this book is to delineate, first, necessary impedimenta according to Church teaching and law as well as the, second, practical obstacles (the negatives) and, conversely, and more importantly, the positive signs of a diaconal vocation. After the barriers are identified, however, one may discover a very large potential field is available for harvest, especially if conversion of the many were to occur. And, perhaps even those who have no impediments but only the practical limitations may discover a means of their reduction. Along the way, of course, there is the smaller plot of those who are potential candidates for the profound ministry of presbyter; it is necessary, then, to make the very important difference between the two ministries, permanent deacon and (permanent, of course) priest, and, as part of the process, their specific, distinct identities.

Ordination Rite

In the ordination rite, the functional faculties of the deacon are mentioned in the suggested homily:

> [Bishop, addressing the people:] This man, your relative and friend, is now to be raised to the order of deacons. Consider carefully the ministry to which he is to be promoted.
>
> He will draw new strength from the gift of the Holy Spirit. He will help the bishop and his body of priests as a minister of the word, of the altar, and of charity. He will make himself a servant of all. As a minister of the altar he will proclaim the Gospel, prepare the sacrifice, and give the Lord's body and blood to the community of believers.
>
> It will also be his duty, at the bishop's discretion, to bring God's word to believer and unbeliever alike, to preside over public prayer, to baptize, to assist at marriages and bless them, to give viaticum to the dying, and to lead the rites of burial. Once he is consecrated by the laying on hands that comes to us from the apostles and is bound more closely to the altar, he will perform works of charity in the name of the bishop or the pastor. From the way he goes about these duties, may you recognize him as a disciple of Jesus, who came to serve, not to be served.
>
> [The bishop, addressing the candidates:]
>
> My sons, you are being raised to the order of deacons. The Lord has set an example for you to follow.
>
> As deacons you will serve Jesus Christ, who was known among his disciples as the one who served others. Do the will of God generously. Serve God and mankind in love and joy. Look upon all unchastity and avarice as worship of false gods; for no man can serve two masters.
>
> Like the men the apostles chose for works of charity, you should be men of good reputation, filled with wisdom and the Holy Spirit. Show before God and mankind that you are

above every suspicion of blame, true ministers of Christ and of God's mysteries, men firmly rooted in faith. Never turn away from the hope which the Gospel offers; now you must not only listen to God's word but also preach it. Hold the mystery of faith with a clear conscience. Express in action what you proclaim by word of mouth. Then the people of Christ, brought to life by the Spirit, will be an offering God accepts. Finally, on the last day, when you go to meet the Lord, you will hear him say: "Well done, good and faithful servant, enter in the joy of your Lord."

The central rite begins:

Bishop: My sons, before you are ordained deacons, you must declare before the people your intention to undertake the office.

Are you willing to be ordained for the Church's ministry by the laying-on-of-hands and the gift of the Holy Spirit?

Together, all the candidates answer: **I am.**

Bishop: Are you resolved to discharge the office of deacon with humility and love in order to assist the bishop and the priests and to serve the people of Christ?

Candidates: **I am.**

Bishop: Are you resolved to hold the mystery of the faith with a clear conscience, as the Apostle urges, and to proclaim this faith in word and action as it is taught by the Gospel and the Church's tradition?

Candidates: **I am.**

Bishop: Are you resolved to maintain and deepen a spirit of prayer appropriate to your way of life and, in keeping with what is required of you, to celebrate faithfully the liturgy of the hours for the Church and for the whole world?

Candidates: **I am.**

Bishop: Are you resolved to shape your way of life always according to the example of Christ, whose body and blood you will give to the people?

Candidates: I am, with the help of God.

PROMISE OF OBEDIENCE

Then each one of the candidates goes to the bishop and, kneeling before him, places his joined hands between those of the bishop...

Bishop: Do you promise respect and obedience to me and my successors?

Candidates: **I do.**

Bishop: May God who has begun the good work in you bring it to fulfillment.

INVITATION TO PRAYER

17. Then all stand, and the bishop, without his miter, invites the people to pray:

My dear people, let us pray that the all-powerful Father will pour out his blessing on these servants of his, whom he receives into the holy order of deacons.

[Assisting] Deacon: **Let us kneel.**

(Candidates lay prostrate)

After the LITANY OF SAINTS:

Bishop: Lord God, Hear our petitions and give your help to this act of your ministry.

We judge these men worthy to serve as deacon and we ask you to bless him

And make him holy. Grant this through Christ our Lord.

R. Amen

Deacon: Let us stand.

LAYING ON OF HANDS

Then all stand. Each candidate goes to the bishop and kneels before him. The bishop lays his hands on the candidates head, in silence.

PRAYER OF CONSECRATION

Each candidate kneels before the bishop. With his hands extended over the candidate, he sings the prayer of consecration.

Almighty God, be present with us by your power.

You are the source of all honor, you assign to each his rank, you give to each his ministry.

You remain unchanged, but you watch over all creation and make it new through your son, Jesus Christ, our Lord: He is your Word, your power, and your wisdom.

You foresee all things in your eternal providence and make due provision for every age. You make the Church, Christ's body, grow to its full stature as a new and greater temple. You enrich it with every kind of grace and perfect it with a diversity of members to serve the whole body in a wonderful pattern of unity.

You established a threefold ministry of worship and service for the glory of your name. As ministers of the tabernacle you chose the sons of Levi and gave them your blessing as their everlasting inheritance.

In the first days of your Church under the inspiration of the Holy Spirit the apostles of your Son appointed seven men of good repute to assist them in the daily ministry, so that they themselves might be more free for prayer and preaching. By prayer and the laying on of the hands the apostles entrusted to those chosen men the ministry of serving at tables.

Lord, look with favor these servants of yours, whom we now dedicate to office of deacon, to minister at your holy altar.

Lord, send forth upon him the Holy Spirit, that he may be strengthened by the gift of sevenfold grace to carry out faithfully the work of the ministry.

May he excel in every virtue: in love that is sincere, in concern for the sick and the poor, in unassuming authority, in self discipline, and in holiness of life. May his conduct exemplify your commandments and lead your people to imitate his purity of life.

May he remain strong and steadfast in Christ, giving to the world the witness of a pure conscience. May he in this life imitate your Son, who came, not to be served but to serve, and one day reign with him in heaven.

We ask this through our Lord Jesus Christ, your Son, who lives and reigns with you and the Holy Spirit, one God, for ever and ever.

R. Amen.

INVESTITURE WITH STOLE AND DALMATIC

PRESENTATION OF THE BOOK OF THE GOSPELS

Vested as a deacon, the newly ordained goes to the bishop and kneels before him. The bishop places the Book of the Gospels in the hands of the newly ordained and says:

Receive the Gospel of Christ, whose herald you have become. Believe what you read, teach what you believe, and practice what you teach.

LITURGY OF THE EUCHARIST

...Father, accept the offering from your whole family and from those you have chosen for the order of deacons. Protect the gifts you have given them, and let them yield a harvest worthy of you.

In any sacrament, there are matter and form. In Baptism, water is the matter, and the pouring of the water, together with the words,

"I baptize you in the name of the Father, and of the Son, and of the Holy Spirit," is the form. In Eucharist, the matter is the bread and wine; the form is the words of institution, said while holding the matter which becomes the Sacred Body and Precious Blood.

In the case of ordination of a deacon, Paul VI stated in *Pontificalis Romani recognitio* (*PRR* – Apostolic Constitution Approving New Rites of Ordination of Deacons, Priests, and Bishops):

> By our supreme apostolic authority we decree and establish the following with regard to the matter and form in the conferring of each order:
>
> In the ordination of deacons, the matter is the laying of the bishop's hands on the individual candidates that is done in silence before the consecratory prayer; the form consists in the words of the consecratory prayer, of which the following belong to the essence and are consequently required for validity:
>
> Lord,
> send forth upon them the Holy Spirit,
> that they be strengthened
> by the gift of your sevenfold grace
> to carry out faithfully the work of the ministry.

The seven *gifts* of the Holy Spirit are wisdom, understanding, counsel, fortitude, knowledge, piety, and fear of the Lord. (*CCE* 1831) The sevenfold grace of the Holy Spirit is taken from Isaiah 11:2-3; according to the Latin Vulgate, which in turn is taken from the Septuagint (Greek) Old Testament. The traditional Douay-Rheims (English) translation is:

> And the Spirit of the Lord shall rest upon him: the spirit of wisdom, and of understanding, the spirit of counsel, and of fortitude, the spirit of knowledge, and of godliness. And he

shall be filled with the spirit of the fear of the Lord. (Isaiah 11:2-3a)

[Footnote comments included in the Haydock Douay-Rheims: St. Jerome: "Christ was filled with his seven gifts, and *of his fullness* his servants *receive*." Thomas Worthington: "Yet all virtues are gifts of the holy Spirit, and the number seven is not specified in the Heb. as the same word (C.) *yirath*, is rendered *godliness*, which (v. 3) means, *fear of the Lord*."]

An English translation from the Hebrew (Revised New American Bible [NABRE], 2011) reads:

> The spirit of the LORD shall rest upon him:
> a spirit of wisdom and of understanding,
> A spirit of counsel and of strength,
> a spirit of knowledge and of fear of the LORD,
> and his delight shall be the fear of the LORD. (Isaiah 11:2-3a)
>
> NABRE Footnote: The source of the traditional names of the gifts of the Holy Spirit. The Septuagint and the Vulgate read "piety" for "fear of the Lord" in its first occurrence, thus listing seven gifts.

The very nature of Orders bestowed on the deacon is the imprint of an additional, indelible character, on top of his Baptism and Confirmation. This character consists of a strengthening by the gift of the sevenfold grace of the Holy Spirit. The grace is also necessary, a precondition for the ministry of priest and bishop, yet, in and of itself is sufficient for the ministry of the deacon.

Contrast the essential component of the diaconal ordination rite with the confirmation rite:

> The bishop faces the people and with hands joined, sings or says:
> My dear friends:
> in Baptism God our Father gave the new birth of eternal life to his chosen sons and daughters.

Let us pray to our Father
that he will pour out the Holy Spirit
to strengthen his sons and daughters with his gifts
and anoint them to be more like Christ the Son of God.
All-powerful God,
 Father of our Lord Jesus Christ,
by water and the Holy Spirit
you freed your sons and daughters from sin
and gave them new life.
 Send your Holy Spirit upon them
to be their Helper and Guide.
 Give them the spirit of wisdom and understanding,
the spirit of right judgment and courage,
the spirit of knowledge and reverence.
 Fill them with the spirit of wonder and awe in your
presence.
 We ask this through Christ our Lord.
 All: Amen.

The essential component in the Latin Rite, according to the Catechism, "is conferred through the anointing with chrism on the forehead, which is done by the laying on of the hand, and through the words: 'Be sealed with the Gift of the Holy Spirit. '" (*CCE* 1300)

The newly confirmed responds:
Amen.
The bishop says:
Peace be with you.
The newly confirmed responds:
And also with you

The sign of peace that concludes the rite of the sacrament signifies and demonstrates ecclesial communion with the bishop and with all the faithful. (*CCE* 1301)

Baptism incorporates the newly baptized into the Church, making them adopted children of God. The Gift of the Spirit in Confirmation, then, brings the *confirmandi* into the fullness of the Church, so as to conform them to be more like Christ, who personifies those very gifts. For the diaconal ordinand, the Rite of Ordination strengthens him for the ministry he is to undertake, thereby conforming him to Christ Jesus, who came not to be served, but to serve.

The identity of the deacon is very much expressed with what he does, as the "who" he has become is empowered to serve. There is almost a sense of the automatic, indeed the ordinary, about the deacon. Everything he is to do – baptize, receive wedding vows, bury the dead, clothe the naked, visit those in prison, bring Communion to the sick, proclaim the Gospel, administer the Chalice – is what is to be the ordinary ministry of the Church. Again, this entire and necessary ministry has been in the custody of the priest for centuries up until Paul VI restored the diaconate; since then it has become differentiated from the priestly, to become more visibly diaconal. Why?

What can a deacon do that a layperson cannot?

In examination of the *munera* of the deacon, the question naturally arises – what's the difference between what a deacon does and what a layperson can do? Conversely, what cannot a layperson legitimately do that a deacon can?

For example, in emergency *any* person can baptize, even someone who is *not* baptized. In the absence of an ordained minister a layperson can be commissioned by the bishop to witness the marriage of a properly prepared man and woman. Similarly, if no priest or deacon is available, a lay person can lead the prayers of the Funeral Rite (Outside of Mass) for the deceased and for those who mourn. Where there is a need, mandated laypeople can serve as extraordinary ministers of Holy Communion (sometimes incorrectly called "Eucharistic ministers"), both within Mass and for taking the consecrated hosts to the sick and homebound.

Similarly, even the deacon cannot minister without being assigned to a particularly ministry, typically a parish, or, in some cases, having at least have the implied permission of the appropriate authority, usually the pastor. So, the deacon has his assignment decree from the bishop as an *ordinary* minister of Holy Communion, for example, while extraordinary ministers have a mandation from the bishop at the request of the pastor.

The list of actions that a deacon can undertake as part of his assigned ministry that a layperson, under no circumstances can legitimately exercise, is limited:

1. Fulfill those items reserved to the deacon, or in his absence, the priest, at Mass:
   a. Be vested in alb, cincture, stole, and dalmatic of appropriate color.
   b. Proclaiming the Gospel, including receiving the blessing of the celebrant, offering the greeting, "The Lord be with you," and receiving the response, "And with your spirit," incensing the Book of the Gospels, stating "A reading from the holy Gospel according to

N.," and closing with "The Gospel of the Lord," accompanied by reverencing the text of the Gospel, with the quiet prayer, "Through the words of the Gospel may our sins be wiped away," or, if a bishop presides, possibly bring the book to andfor him to reverence.

c. Preparing the chalice with wine and water, accompanied by the quiet prayer, "By the mystery of this water and wine may we come to share in the divinity of Christ who humbled himself to share in our humanity."

d. Remain standing during the Eucharistic Prayer; kneeling (if able) from the Epiclesis through the elevation of the chalice after the words of institution.

e. At the end of the Eucharistic Prayer, elevate the chalice during the doxology (Through Him, with Him, in Him...) and Great Amen.

f. Inviting the exchange of the sign of peace: "Let us offer each other the sign of peace."

g. Assisting with the fraction rite, if needed.

h. After Communion, purification of the sacred vessels.

i. For the dismissal, one of four options: "Go forth, the Mass is ended," "Go and announce the Gospel of the Lord," "Go in peace, glorifying the Lord by your life," or "Go in peace."

2. The deacon may offer blessings of persons and objects with inclusion of the Sign of the Cross, in the name of the Church, as provided in the Book of Blessings. (Lay persons may lead designated prayers of blessing, but without those parts reserved to the ordained.)

3. The deacon or priest presides over the full Rite of Baptism of Children, including the two anointings (Oil of the Catechumens and of the Chrism), blessing of the water, the Ephphatha blessing of the ears (Mark 7:34) and mouth, and the final blessings of the mother, father, and assembly, including the Sign of the Cross.

4. The deacon or priest, if presiding over other liturgical and paraliturgical rites, offers the final blessing with the Sign of the Cross. For example, the Liturgy of the Hours concludes with the priest or deacon offering the same blessing and dismissal as Mass, while a layperson would conclude the Liturgy of the Hours by saying "May the Lord bless us, protect us from all evil and bring us to everlasting life," while making the sign of the cross over himself or herself.
5. Wear clerical garb according to diocesan norms.

Other than these particular items, the principal difference between the actions of the deacon and those of a layperson who may have temporary deputation to receive wedding vows or distribute Holy Communion is indicated by the title of the latter functionary: *extraordinary* minister of Holy Communion. The deacon, along with priest and bishop, is an *ordinary* minister. The term "ordinary" has several connotations beyond those we use familiarly in conversation. As an adjective, there are two relevant senses: "routine" or "usual" are synonyms of the first sense. Thus, in the normal, *ordinary* course of things, a deacon or priest would baptize and infant within the established rites in his assigned parish. The second sense, "having or constituting immediate or original jurisdiction," is in a limited way pertinent to the deacon. As a noun, "ordinary" refers to "a prelate exercising original jurisdiction over a specified territory or group." In other words, the governing bishop of a diocese is its ordinary; an auxiliary bishop is not an ordinary. . . . The deacon is delegated to have jurisdiction in those *munera* which he has been given; thusly is the deacon an ordinary minister. *Ordinarily*, then, the minister of baptism or funeral rite is a deacon or priest. There is an *order* within the church, to which sacred ministers are *ordained* to serve. Occasionally, extraordinary circumstances arise which require extraordinary responses, for example, extraordinary ministers of Holy Communion, or emergency lay minister of baptism. In the latter case, the core action and words of the rite are performed: As the [pure] water is poured over the head, the minister says, "I baptize you in the name of the Father, and of the Son, and of the Holy Spirit." If and when the opportunity presents itself, when the newly baptized has recovered health, the rest of the rites of Baptism are then supplied by an ordinary minister – a deacon or priest.

The functional distinctions between laity and deacons, then, are the differences of ordinary versus extraordinary, and, in effect, completeness and incompleteness of liturgical actions. However, there is still something more, in the grace of ordination itself: the strengthening of the sevenfold grace of the Holy Spirit described above. But, what does this accomplish; what does it mean?

Ministry of the laity

The principal documents of Vatican Council II are the four Constitutions on the Sacred Liturgy (*Sacrosanctum Concilium*), the Church (*Lumen Gentium*), Divine Revelation (*Dei Verbum*), and the Church in the Modern World (*Gaudium et spes*). The other documents complement and/or flow from the primary texts. *Lumen Gentium*, in particular, introduces some of the dominant themes of the Council, especially the universal call to holiness. Quoting the Gospels (Matthew 5:48, Mark 12:30) and Paul's letters (Ephesians 5:3, Colossians 3:12),

> Thus it is evident to everyone, that all the faithful of Christ of whatever rank or status, are called to the fullness of the Christian life and to the perfection of charity; by this holiness as such a more human manner of living is promoted in this earthly society. (*LG* 40, ¶2).

Further, the entire Church is not only called to holiness, it is obligated to serve all:

> Inspired by no earthly ambition, the Church seeks but a solitary goal: to carry forward the work of Christ under the lead of the befriending Spirit. And Christ entered this world to give witness to the truth, to rescue and not to sit in judgment, to serve and not to be served [Matthew 20:28]. (*GS* 3, ¶2).

The call to holiness and the obligation to serve are inseparable and are a consequence of the first sacrament, Baptism. Immediately after baptism of an infant, the child is anointed:

> The *anointing with sacred chrism*, perfumed oil consecrated by the bishop, signifies the gift of the Holy Spirit to the newly baptized, who has become a Christian, that is, one "anointed" by the Holy Spirit, incorporated into Christ who is anointed priest, prophet, and king. (*CCE* 1241).

Two paragraphs of *Apostolicam Actuositatem* [*AA*] emphasize the distinctive role of the laity in the Church and world today:

In the Church there is a diversity of ministry but a oneness of mission. Christ conferred on the Apostles and their successors the duty of teaching, sanctifying, and ruling in His name and power. But the laity likewise share in the priestly, prophetic, and royal office of Christ and therefore have their own share in the mission of the whole people of God in the Church and in the world.

They exercise the apostolate in fact by their activity directed to the evangelization and sanctification of men and to the penetrating and perfecting of the temporal order through the spirit of the Gospel. In this way, their temporal activity openly bears witness to Christ and promotes the salvation of men. Since the laity, in accordance with their state of life, live in the midst of the world and its concerns, they are called by God to exercise their apostolate in the world like leaven, with the ardor of the spirit of Christ. (*AA* 2, ¶3-4).

It is from among lay men who are actively fulfilling their distinctive Christian apostolate that permanent deacons are called. However, in exploring the calls of the laity, it is fair to ask why a layman, who already is attempting to live out his baptismal call, should be further called to the diaconate.

In the citation above, reference is made to the successors of the apostles who are entrusted with the "office of teaching, sanctifying, and governing." Lay people are not sharers in the official ministry of the ordained, but, rather, share in the three-fold, non-ordained office of Christ, priest, prophet, and king, in their own apostolate. Laypersons, as well as clergy and religious have both rights and duties to be apostles. An apostle is one who is sent by the Lord himself. In action they offer spiritual sacrifices and bear witness to Christ.

Charity, what *AA* calls "the soul of the apostolate," is received and nurtured by the sacraments, especially Eucharist. To bring the Gospel message of salvation to the whole world is the purpose of the Church and the noble obligation of all Christians. To experience the apostolate, the Holy Spirit, in addition to sanctifying the People of God (the Church), gives each of the faithful special gifts." To each individual the manifestation of the Spirit is given for some benefit." (1 Corinthians 12) Such gifts, "charisms" from the Greek, include the expression of wisdom or knowledge, faith, healing, mighty deeds, prophesy, discernment of spirits, varieties of tongues, or interpretation of tongues (1 Corinthians 12:8-10).

The exercise of the gifts of the Spirit is to build up the Body of Christ, the Church, and should always be subject to pastoral guidance: "Do not quench the Spirit. Do not despise prophetic utterances. Test everything; retain what is good." (1 Thessalonians 5:19-21) The lay apostolate is to be a leaven for the world – in the workplace, home, and Public Square. The committed lay person participates in civic activities, especially voting and communication of legitimate concerns to public officials. Some may be led to stand for public office; their Catholic faith is expected to permeate their campaigns and service, if elected, as a witness to the power of honesty, integrity, charity, and respect for the common good, protection of the weak and powerless, more particularly the unborn and elderly.

Qualified lay persons are expected to provide guidance to their pastors in matters regarding prudent usage of the temporal goods of the Church. Similarly, pastors, assisted by deacons and other priests, are to provide the spiritual goods, both Word and Sacrament, to guide, sanctify, and nourish the faithful in their daily apostolate of service to family, work, and civic responsibilities.

While the work of redemption in Christ is essentially salvific, it also includes the renewal of the world. The Gospel message is the preeminent mission of the Church, accompanied by the need to penetrate the contemporary world in which we all live. The lay Christian is active in both domains as a believer living in this time and place; he or she is a single person, a single soul, with one Christian conscience, even if married.

The apostolate is to proclaim and communicate the message and grace of Christ. This mission, entrusted first to the clergy, also includes a central role for the laity, as they have "innumerable opportunities ... for the exercise of their apostolate of evangelization and sanctification." (*AA* 6, ¶2) First, there is the witness of a Christian life and, then being on the lookout for opportunities to proclaim Christ in word and action. Lay Christians play a critical role in explaining and defending the core of the Gospel message and its relevance and application to the present time, in family, culture, economy, workplace, political action, and even in international relations.

A vibrant lay apostolate is the seed bed of religious vocation. Out of faithful families and devout family life, young men for centuries have and continue to hear the call to the altar of sacrifice. And, now, mature men, married or celibate, hear a revitalized invitation to the service of the Church, sacramentalized – the permanent diaconate.

In a mysterious way, the faithful service of a lay catechist becomes strengthened by the consecration of Holy Orders, thereby becoming even more fruitful through a greater outpouring of the sevenfold gifts of the Holy Spirit. Confirmation, whereby the gifts are first received, is not the end of God's generosity, for he continues to pour forth charismatic gifts to those who ask for them, that they may better fulfill their apostolic charge. Then, for those men with a vocational call, the sacramental grace of ordination is supplied by the laying-on-of-hands by the bishop. The charismatic gifts bestowed on the confirmed and the strengthening of the sevenfold gifts of the Spirit via diaconal ordination are not ordered primarily for the individual confirmand or ordinand but for those whom they are to serve. All of the sacraments are sanctifying, but sanctification extends beyond the individual, for it is to orient the person towards the service of God and neighbor.

In her *Interior Castle* [IC] St. Teresa of Avila wrote:

It is of the utmost importance for the beginner to associate with those who lead a spiritual life and not only with those in the same mansion as herself, but with others who have travelled farther into the castle, who will aid her greatly and draw her to join them. (IC 12)

In other words, by seeking sanctification, a closer relationship with God, the individual Christian draws others to God.

Given all the dimensions of the lay apostolate, why should a devout layman consider going beyond the apostolate and consider the vocation of the diaconate? As noted above, the Fathers of Vatican II wrote in *Ad Gentes*: "It is only right to strengthen them by the imposition of hands ... that they may carry out their ministry more effectively because of the sacramental grace of the diaconate" (AG 16, 6). . . . It is this statement that is a primary motivation for this book.

There are many laymen active as catechists – lay university and seminary professors, youth ministers, directors of religious education, newspaper and magazine columnists, leaders of Catholic charity and outreach organizations, evangelization leaders...) who have not yet heard or responded to the call to be deacons. (Or they are convinced that they do not have such a vocation.)Imagine what grace might be received by the Church should these men be strengthened by ordination in the apostolates in which they are already working!

Priest versus deacon? No, Priest and deacon

Some, in describing the restored diaconate, may have used a metaphor, "the deacon is a bridge between laity and clergy." However, whether prompted or not, the metaphor may then have been modified slightly to become "... bridge between laity and priests," as, after all, deacons are themselves clergy, so how could one be a bridge to the very same bridge? But, even a "bridge to priests" is inapt, for several reasons: the priest retains his own diaconal character even as he receives the character of the presbyter with his presbyteral ordination; so, again, he would be his own bridge. Further, the deacon, while serving at the altar, is not serving the priest; rather he is serving *with* the priest, both having been sent by the bishop; at the beginning of Mass both priest and deacon reverence the altar. . . .

The liturgy of the Mass, the source and summit of the Christian life, typifies the difference between priest and deacon. The priest presides at Mass, *in persona Christi* (in the person of Christ – this terminology is explored in depth below) and offers exclusive prayers, especially the Eucharistic Prayer. The Prayer incorporates the words of institution by which bread and wine are transubstantiated into the Lord's body and blood. There are those other prayers, both audible and quiet, which are reserved to him, including the collect, doxology, and final blessing. (In the absence of the deacon: the priest also proclaims the Gospel, elevates the chalice at the end of the Eucharistic Prayer, invites the sign of peace, and offers the dismissal, while a lay person or the priest offers the intercessions – prayers of the faithful – and the acolyte prepares the altar.)

In the liturgy, according to the General Instruction of the Roman Missal and directives (rubrics) with the Missal the priest wears alb (white vestment), cincture (rope belt), priest's stole around the neck, and *chasuble.* The deacon wears alb, cincture, stole over the left shoulder, and *dalmatic.* During the Liturgy of the Word, the deacon and priest stand and sit at the same times, except, of course during the homily, whether given by priest or deacon. The deacon requests the blessing of the celebrant prior to proclaiming the Gospel; if the priest proclaims the Gospel, he prays a quiet prayer before moving to the ambo. The preparation of the altar may be undertaken by the deacon and the priest together, or the priest remains seated. Typically, the priest, assisted by the deacon and acolytes, receives the gifts, although the deacon may receive the gifts while the celebrant remains seated.

During the preparation of the gifts, the deacon hands the bread to the celebrant, and, before giving him the wine in the chalice, adds a small amount of water to the wine, while saying quietly, "By the mystery of this water and wine may we come to share in the divinity of Christ who humbled himself to share in our humanity."

At the beginning of the Eucharistic Prayer, the deacon remains standing. He (unless physically limited) kneels beginning with the Epiclesis (invocation of the Holy Spirit), which is different in each Eucharistic Prayer:

I. Be pleased, O God, we pray, to bless, acknowledge, and approve this offering in every respect; make it spiritual and acceptable, so that it may become for us the Body and Blood of your most beloved Son, our Lord Jesus Christ.	II. Make holy, therefore, these gifts, we pray, by sending down your Spirit upon them like the dewfall, so that they may become for us the Body and Blood of our Lord Jesus Christ.
III. Therefore, O Lord, we humbly implore you: by the same Spirit graciously make holy these gifts we have brought to you for consecration, that they may become the Body and Blood of your Son our Lord Jesus Christ	IV. Therefore, O Lord, we pray: may this same Holy Spirit graciously sanctify these offerings, that they may become= the Body and Blood of our Lord Jesus Christ

(The epiclesis over the gifts of bread and wine, while the deacon kneels, may remind him of the epiclesis at his ordination, invoked by the bishop while he, as a candidate, knelt.) After the words of institution over the bread, the priest elevates the host, then after placing it back on the paten and corporal, genuflects. After the words of institution over the wine, the priest elevates the chalice, then after placing it back on the corporal, genuflects. As he rises the second time, the deacon also rises and remains standing through the rest of the Eucharistic Prayer alongside the priest. Concelebrating priests and the deacons (if standing) bow to the altar each of the two times that the principal celebrant genuflects during the Eucharistic Prayer. The kneeling deacon does not bow his head when the celebrant genuflects; his posture already conveys reverence. The other time the celebrant genuflects, prior to his own self-communion, is not accompanied by bows of the concelebrants or deacons.

At the end of the Eucharistic Prayer, the priest elevates the Sacred Body while the deacon elevates the chalice. The deacon offers the Sign of Peace. While it is desirable that all of the hosts be those consecrated at the Mass, it is not unusual for a surplus of hosts to be reserved in the Tabernacle. At the *Agnus Dei* (Lamb of God), the deacon (or in his absence the priest) goes to the Tabernacle for the ciboria which contain the additional, previously consecrated, hosts (unless the Tabernacle is located apart from the sanctuary, in which case an extraordinary minister may bring the other ciboria to the deacon).

The priest celebrant self-communicates (consuming the consecrated host and drinking from the chalice); the deacon receives the host and chalice from the priest in the same way as each communicant in the assembly (in the United States, the communicant, including the deacon, bows the head before saying "Amen," and receiving first the host and, repeating the same, receives from the chalice).

The priest offers or leads virtually all of the prayers from the Collect at the beginning, through the preparation of the gifts, the Eucharistic Prayer, the Communion Rite, the prayer after Communion, and the final blessing. The deacon may introduce the blessing if it is a solemn one ("Bow down for the blessing."); after the final blessing, the deacon dismisses the people.

47

To summarize, at Mass, the deacon complements the actions of the priest. In the absence of the deacon, some of his roles are taken by the reader or acolyte, while others are taken by the priest, either celebrant or concelebrant.

The deacon is especially identified with the proclamation of the Gospel, after which he prays quietly, "Through the words of the Gospel may our sins be wiped away." The deacon may offer the third Penitential Act after its introduction by the priest, such as "You were sent to heal the contrite of heart..." Since the deacon elevates the chalice at the end of the Eucharistic Prayer and is designated by the *GIMR* to minister the chalice during Communion, when both species are offered, it is worthwhile to focus on the specific words of institution of the Eucharist, both the Sacred Body and those over the chalice of the Precious Blood. The deacon (or priest in the absence of a deacon) adds water to the wine at the preparation of the gifts, saying "By the mystery of this water and wine..."

Over the bread, the priest repeats the words of Jesus:

> Take this, all of you, and eat of it,
> for this is my Body,
> which will be given up for you.

The words of institution spoken over the chalice read:

> Take this all of you, and drink from it, for this is the chalice of my Blood, the Blood of the new and eternal covenant, which will be poured out for you and for many for the forgiveness of sins. Do this in memory of me.

Somehow, then the deacon, along with the priest, confronts both the mystery of the Incarnation and forgiveness of sins, in "the blood of the new and eternal covenant ... poured out for many for the forgiveness of sins." The deacon is like the servants who prepared the jugs of water at the wedding at Cana (John 2:5-7), or Andrew who found the boy with a few loaves and fishes which the Lord multiplied (John 6:9), or the two disciples (Mark 14:13; Peter and John, according to Luke 22:8) who prepared the Passover meal.

The priest and bishop are the only ministers of the Sacraments of Reconciliation, Anointing of the Sick, and Confirmation. Normally, Confirmation is reserved to the bishop except for those who are received into the Church at the Easter Vigil Mass (a priest celebrant or concelebrant confirms in this case), or by delegation to priests in certain other circumstances. Orders are bestowed by the bishop for deacons and priests by his authority, and by (usually) archbishops for bishops, under the authority of the Holy Father.

Only a priest may be a pastor or a chaplain. The bishop is the shepherd of his diocese, while assigned priests are shepherds of their parishes. Should a deacon be given administrative responsibility for a parish in the absence of a priest in the parish, there is still to be an assigned priest who has pastoral responsibility for that parish.

Only a priest acts *in persona Christi,* when administering the sacraments, especially the Eucharist. And, only a bishop or priest acts in the person of Christ the Head (*in persona Christi Capitis*), as pastor of his diocese or parish. (See the next section for elaboration on these two points.)

As priest and bishop received the *munera* (delegated responsibilities) of the deacon upon their own diaconal ordination, so when they exercise those *munera,* such as baptizing, preaching, and receiving wedding vows, they minister out of and through their own diaconal ordination as well as their subsequent ordinations. This is intrinsic to ordination, as the rites, beginning with the diaconate, bestow an irrevocable, distinct character on the recipient.

Bishop and priest act *in persona Christi* – What about the deacon?

The Latin phrases, *in persona Christi*, and *in persona Christi Capitis*¸ have been the subject of some controversy in recent years, relative to the distinct identities of the deacon and the priest. Does a deacon, like a priest, act (1) *in persona Christi Capitis* (in the person of Christ the head) or (2) simply *in persona Christi*, or (3) not at all in the person of Christ?

In *Lumen Gentium*, the principal document of Vatican Council II, the bishops wrote (**emphasis** added):

> Christ, whom the Father has sanctified and sent into the world, has through His apostles, made their successors, the bishops, partakers of His consecration and His mission. They have legitimately handed on to different individuals in the Church various degrees of participation in this ministry. Thus the divinely established ecclesiastical ministry is exercised on different levels by those who from antiquity have been called bishops, priests and deacons. **Priests**, although they do not possess the highest degree of the priesthood, and although they are dependent on the bishops in the exercise of their power, nevertheless they are united with the bishops in sacerdotal dignity. By the power of the sacrament of Orders, in the image of Christ the eternal high Priest, they are consecrated to preach the Gospel and shepherd the faithful and to celebrate divine worship, so that they are true priests of the New Testament. Partakers of the function of Christ the sole Mediator, on their level of ministry, they announce the divine word to all. They exercise their sacred function especially in the Eucharistic worship or the celebration of the Mass by which acting **in the person of Christ** and proclaiming His Mystery they unite the prayers of the faithful with the sacrifice of their Head and renew and apply in the sacrifice of the Mass until the coming of the

Lord the only sacrifice of the New Testament namely that of Christ offering Himself once for all a spotless Victim to the Father. For the sick and the sinners among the faithful, they exercise the ministry of alleviation and reconciliation and they present the needs and the prayers of the faithful to God the Father. Exercising within the limits of their authority the function of **Christ as Shepherd and Head**, they gather together God's family as a brotherhood all of one mind, and lead them in the Spirit, through Christ, to God the Father. In the midst of the flock they adore Him in spirit and in truth. Finally, they labor in word and doctrine, believing what they have read and meditated upon in the law of God, teaching what they have believed, and putting in practice in their own lives what they have taught. (*LG 21*)

At a lower level of the hierarchy are **deacons**, upon whom hands are imposed "not unto the priesthood, but unto a ministry of service". For strengthened by sacramental grace, in communion with the bishop and his group of priests they serve in the diaconate of the liturgy, of the word, and of charity to the people of God. (*LG 29*)

The issue arose when the 1983 Code of Canon Law stated:

Canon 1008: By divine institution some among the Christian faithful are constituted sacred ministers through the sacrament of orders by means of the indelible character with which they are marked; accordingly they are consecrated and deputed to shepherd the people of God, each in accord with his own grade of orders, by fulfilling **in the person of Christ the head** [Latin: *in persona Christi Capitis*] the functions of teaching, sanctifying and governing.

Canon 1009: 1. The orders are the episcopacy, the presbyterate, and the diaconate. 2. They are conferred by an imposition of hands and by the consecratory prayer which the liturgical books prescribe for the individual grades.

Lumen Gentium does not include deacons with the attribute *in persona Christi*, while the *CIC* appears to.

Section 875 of the first edition (1994) of the *CCE* seems to follow Canon 1008:

> No one can bestow grace on himself; it must be given and offered. This fact presupposes ministers of grace, authorized and empowered by Christ. From him, they receive the mission and faculty ('the sacred power') to act *in persona Christi Capitis.* The ministry in which Christ's emissaries do and give by God's grace what they cannot do and give by their own powers, is called a "sacrament" by the Church's tradition. Indeed, the ministry of the Church is conferred by a special sacrament.

In 1997 the "definitive" edition of the *CCE* included several changes from the 1994 version. Perhaps the most significant change inthe was to Section 875:

> No one can bestow grace on himself; it must be given and offered. This fact presupposes ministers of grace, authorized and empowered by Christ. From him, bishops and priests receive the mission and faculty ("the sacred power") to act *in persona Christi Capitis*; deacons receive the strength to serve the people of God in the *diakonia* of liturgy, word, and charity, in communion with the bishop and his presbyterate. The ministry in which Christ's emissaries do and give by God's grace what they cannot do and give by their own powers, is called a "sacrament" by the Church's tradition. Indeed, the ministry of the Church is conferred by a special sacrament."

In 2009 Pope Benedict XVI issued a short Apostolic Letter, *Omnium in Mentum*, *Motu Proprio* (by his own authority), which modified the text of two canons in the Code of Canon Law relative to the three degrees of Orders. . . .

The letter provides the reasoning behind the change, to make Canon Law clearly consistent with Church teaching as defined by Vatican Council II:

> First, in can. 1008 and can. 1009 of the *Code of Canon Law*, on the sacrament of Holy Orders, the essential distinction between the common priesthood of the faithful and the ministerial priesthood is reaffirmed, while the difference between the episcopate, the presbyterate and the diaconate is made clear. Inasmuch as my venerable Predecessor John Paul II, after consulting the Fathers of the Congregation for the Doctrine of the Faith, ordered that the text of n. 1581 of the *Catechism of the Catholic Church* be modified in order better to convey the teaching on deacons found in the Dogmatic Constitution *Lumen Gentium* of the Second Vatican Council (n. 29), I have determined that the canonical norm concerning this subject should likewise be adjusted. Consequently, after hearing the view of the Pontifical Council for Legislative Texts, I decree that the words of the aforementioned canons are to be modified as set forth below.

The changes in the two canons, 1008 and 1009, resolve an apparent discrepancy between Vatican Council II's *LG* and the 1997 ("definitive") Catechism of the Catholic Church on one hand and the 1983*CIC* on the other. The International Theological Commission articulated the conflict in 2003 (English version, 2004) in their book "From the *Diakonia* of Christ to the *Diakonia* of the Apostles," and anticipated the change to the Code (in the book's footnotes). At the heart of the conflict is the question of the applicability of the term *"in persona Christi capitis"* to not only bishops and priests, but also to deacons. *LG* and the 1997 Catechism limit the term to only bishops and priests while the 1983 Code implies that the term applies to deacons as well. The first edition of the Catechism was more consistent with the 1983 Code than with *Lumen Gentium*. One of the principal changes from the 1994 to the 1997 (definitive) Catechism restored consistency with *Lumen Gentium*; with that change the *CIC* became a singular outlier. The *Motu Proprio* achieves consistency among all three magisterial documents in regard to this particular teaching.

The 1983 *CIC* (English translation from the Vatican website) reads:

> Canon 1008: By divine institution some among the Christian faithful are constituted sacred ministers through the sacrament of orders by means of the indelible character with which they are marked; accordingly they are consecrated and deputed to shepherd the people of God, each in accord with his own grade of orders, by fulfilling in the person of Christ the head [Latin: *in persona Christi Capitis*] the functions of teaching, sanctifying and governing.

> Canon 1009: 1. The orders are the episcopacy, the presbyterate, and the diaconate. 2. They are conferred by an imposition of hands and by the consecratory prayer which the liturgical books prescribe for the individual grades.

Section 875 of the first edition of the Catechism of the Catholic Church (English, 1994) seems to follow Canon 1008:

> No one can bestow grace on himself; it must be given and offered. This fact presupposes ministers of grace, authorized and empowered by Christ. From him, they receive the mission and faculty ('the sacred power') to act *in persona Christi Capitis*. The ministry in which Christ's emissaries do and give by God's grace what they cannot do and give by their own powers, is called a "sacrament" by the Church's tradition. Indeed, the ministry of the Church is conferred by a special sacrament.

The corresponding section of the second edition of the Catechism (English, 1997), which, according to the *Motu Proprio* was changed at the direction of John Paul II, now reads:

> No one can bestow grace on himself; it must be given and offered. This fact presupposes ministers of grace, authorized and empowered by Christ. From him, bishops and priests receive the mission and faculty ("the sacred power") to act *in persona Christi Capitis*; deacons receive the strength to serve the people of God in the *diakonia* of liturgy, word, and charity, in communion with the bishop and his presbyterate. The ministry in which Christ's emissaries do and give by God's grace what they cannot do and give by their own powers, is called a "sacrament" by the Church's tradition. Indeed, the ministry of the Church is conferred by a special sacrament."

The latter expression (in the second edition of the *CCE*) is more consistent with what was written by the Fathers at Vatican Council II (in LG, **emphasis** added):

> Christ, whom the Father has sanctified and sent into the world, has through His apostles, made their successors, the bishops, partakers of His consecration and His mission. They have legitimately handed on to different individuals in the Church various degrees of participation in this ministry. Thus the divinely established ecclesiastical ministry is exercised on different levels by those who from antiquity have been called bishops, priests and deacons. **Priests**, although they do not possess the highest degree of the priesthood, and although they are dependent on the bishops in the exercise of their power, nevertheless they are united with the bishops in sacerdotal dignity. By the power of the sacrament of Orders, in the image of Christ the eternal high Priest, they are consecrated to preach the Gospel and shepherd the faithful and to celebrate divine worship, so that they are

true priests of the New Testament. Partakers of the function of Christ the sole Mediator, on their level of ministry, they announce the divine word to all. They exercise their sacred function especially in the Eucharistic worship or the celebration of the Mass by which acting **in the person of Christ** and proclaiming His Mystery they unite the prayers of the faithful with the sacrifice of their Head and renew and apply in the sacrifice of the Mass until the coming of the Lord the only sacrifice of the New Testament namely that of Christ offering Himself once for all a spotless Victim to the Father. For the sick and the sinners among the faithful, they exercise the ministry of alleviation and reconciliation and they present the needs and the prayers of the faithful to God the Father. Exercising within the limits of their authority the function of **Christ as Shepherd and Head**, they gather together God's family as a brotherhood all of one mind, and lead them in the Spirit, through Christ, to God the Father. In the midst of the flock they adore Him in spirit and in truth. Finally, they labor in word and doctrine, believing what they have read and meditated upon in the law of God, teaching what they have believed, and putting in practice in their own lives what they have taught. (*LG 21*)

At a lower level of the hierarchy are **deacons**, upon whom hands are imposed "not unto the priesthood, but unto a ministry of service". For strengthened by sacramental grace, in communion with the bishop and his group of priests they serve in the diaconate of the liturgy, of the word, and of charity to the people of God. (*LG 29*)

From Benedict XVI's *Motu Proprio*, the English translation of the changed canons in the *CIC* reads:

Title VI. Orders

Can. 1008 By divine institution, the sacrament of orders establishes some among the Christian faithful as sacred ministers through an indelible character which marks them. They are consecrated and designated, each according to his grade, so that they may serve the People of God by a new and specific title.

Can. 1009 §1 The orders are the **episcopate**, the **presbyterate**, and the **diaconate**.
§2. They are conferred by the imposition of hands and the consecratory prayer which the liturgical books prescribe for the individual grades.
§3. Those who are constituted in the order of the **episcopate** or the **presbyterate** receive the mission and capacity to act **in the person of Christ the Head**, whereas **deacons** are empowered to serve the People of God in the ministries of the liturgy, the word, and charity.

Can "*in persona Christi*", with or without "*capitis*", be applied to the identity and/or action of the deacon? With the changes in the *CCE* and *CIC* I have yet to find an example in any other magisterial document issued before or since, of such an application. A search among formal and informal Church documents issued over the past seven decades indicates, more typically, "*in persona Christi*" alone (without "*Capitis*"), also appears to be limited to the ministry of the priest and bishop, especially in relationship to the peak moment of the Liturgy, the words of institution within the Eucharistic Prayer. A selection of papal documents with the terminology as applied to priests (**emphasis** added) is provided here:

Pius XII, *Mediator Dei,* Encyclical, 1947 (Issued, of course, before the restoration of the permanent diaconate):

40. Only to the apostles, and thenceforth to those on whom their successors have imposed hands, is granted the power of the priesthood, in virtue of which they represent **the**

person of Jesus Christ before their people, acting at the same time as representatives of their people before God....

68. The august sacrifice of the altar, then, is no mere empty commemoration of the passion and death of Jesus Christ, but a true and proper act of sacrifice, whereby the High Priest by an unbloody immolation offers Himself a most acceptable victim to the Eternal Father, as He did upon the cross." It is one and the same victim; the same person now offers it by the ministry of His priests, who then offered Himself on the cross, the manner of offering alone being different."

69. The priest is the same, Jesus Christ, **whose sacred Person His minister represents**. Now the minister, by reason of the sacerdotal consecration which he has received, is made like to the High Priest and possesses the power of performing actions **in virtue of Christ's very person.**

Paul VI, *Sacredotal Caelibatus,* Encyclical, 1967

29. ... acting **in the person of Christ**, the priest unites himself most intimately with the offering, and places on the altar his entire life, which bears the marks of the holocaust.

John Paul II, *Dominicae Cenae*, Apostolic Exhortation, 1980

8. The priest offers the holy Sacrifice *in persona Christi*... Awareness of this reality throws a certain light on the character and significance of the priest celebrant who, by confecting the holy Sacrifice and acting *"in persona Christi,"* is sacramentally (and ineffably) brought into that most profound sacredness, and made part of it, spiritually linking with it in turn all those participating in the eucharistic assembly.

What in the Letter to the Galatians Paul describes as a simple "fact" of Baptism – the gift of new being – he presents to us in the Letter to the Ephesians as an ongoing task: "Put off your old nature which belongs to your former manner of life. . . and [you must] put on the new nature, created after the likeness of God in true righteousness and holiness. Therefore, putting away falsehood, let everyone speak the truth with his neighbour, for we are members of one another. Be angry but do not sin..." (Eph 4: 22-26).

This theology of Baptism returns in a new way and with a new insistence in priestly Ordination.

Just as in Baptism an "exchange of clothing" is given, an exchanged destination, a new existential communion with Christ, so also in priesthood there is an exchange: in the administration of the sacraments, the priest now acts and speaks "*in persona Christi*". In the sacred mysteries, he does not represent himself and does not speak expressing himself, but speaks for the Other, for Christ.

Thus, in the Sacraments, he dramatically renders visible what being a priest means in general; what we have expressed with our "*Adsum* – I am ready", during our consecration to the priesthood: I am here so that you may make use of me. We put ourselves at the disposal of the One who "died for all, that those who live might live no longer for themselves..." (II Cor 5: 15). Putting ourselves at Christ's disposal means that we allow ourselves to be attracted within his "for all": in being with him we can truly be "for all".

In persona Christi: at the moment of priestly Ordination, the Church has also made this reality of "new clothes" visible and comprehensible to us externally through being clothed in liturgical vestments.

Benedict XVI, General Audience, Saint Peter's Square Wednesday, 14 April 2010

> In this Easter Season that brings us to Pentecost and also ushers us into the celebrations for the closure of the Year for Priests, scheduled for this coming 9-11 June, I am eager to devote a few more reflections to the topic of the ordained Ministry, elaborating on the fruitful realities of the priest's configuration to **Christ the Head** in the exercise of the *tria munera* that he receives: namely, the three offices of teaching, sanctifying and governing.

In order to understand what it means for the priest to act *in persona Christi Capitis* in the person of Christ the Head and to realize what consequences derive from the duty of representing the Lord, especially in the exercise of these three offices, it is necessary first of all to explain what "representation" means. The priest represents Christ. What is implied by "representing" someone? In ordinary language it usually means being delegated by someone to be present in his place, to speak and act in his stead because the person he represents is absent from the practical action. Let us ask ourselves: does the priest represent the Lord in this way? The answer is no, because in the Church Christ is never absent, the Church is his living Body and he is the Head of the Church, present and active within her. Christ is never absent, on the contrary he is present in a way that is untrammeled by space and time through the event of the Resurrection that we contemplate in a special way in this Easter Season.

Therefore the priest, who acts *in persona Christi Capitis* and representing the Lord, never acts in the name of someone who is absent but, rather, **in the very Person of the Risen Christ**, who makes himself present with his truly effective action. He really acts today and brings about what the priest would be incapable of: the consecration of the wine and the bread so that they may really be the Lord's presence, the absolution of sins. The Lord makes his own action present in the person who carries out these gestures. These three duties of the priest which Tradition has identified in the Lord's different words about mission: teaching, sanctifying and governing in their difference and in their deep unity are a specification of this effective representation. In fact, they are the three actions of the Risen Christ, the same that he teaches today, in the Church and in the world. Thereby he creates faith, gathers together his people, creates the presence of truth and really builds the communion of the universal Church; and sanctifies and guides.

Benedict XVI, *Sacramentum Caritatis*, Post-Synodal Apostolic Exhortation, February 22, 2007

> The Eucharist and the Sacrament of Holy Orders, In persona Christi capitis
>
> 23. The intrinsic relationship between the Eucharist and the sacrament of Holy Orders clearly emerges from Jesus' own words in the Upper Room: "Do this in memory of me" (Lk 22:19). On the night before he died, Jesus instituted the Eucharist and at the same time established the priesthood of the New Covenant. He is priest, victim and altar: the mediator between God the Father and his people (cf. Heb 5:5-10), the victim of atonement (cf. 1 Jn 2:2, 4:10) who offers himself on the altar of the Cross. No one can say "this is my body" and "this is the cup of my blood" except **in the name and in the person of Christ**, the one high priest of the new and eternal Covenant (cf. Heb 8-9). Earlier meetings of the Synod of Bishops had considered the question of the ordained priesthood, both with regard to the nature of the ministry and the formation of candidates. Here, in the light of the discussion that took place during the last Synod, I consider it important to recall several important points about the relationship between the sacrament of the Eucharist and Holy Orders. First of all, we need to stress once again that the connection between Holy Orders and

the Eucharist is seen most clearly at Mass, when the Bishop or priest presides **in the person of Christ the Head**.

The Church teaches that priestly ordination is the indispensable condition for the valid celebration of the Eucharist. Indeed, "in the ecclesial service of the ordained minister, it is Christ himself who is present to his Church as Head of his Body, Shepherd of his flock, High Priest of the redemptive sacrifice." [*CCE* 1548] Certainly the ordained minister also acts "in the name of the whole Church, when presenting to God the prayer of the Church, and above all when offering the eucharistic sacrifice." [*CCE* 1552] As a result, priests should be conscious of the fact that in their ministry they must never put themselves or their personal opinions in first place, but Jesus Christ. Any attempt to make themselves the centre of the liturgical action contradicts their very identity as priests. The priest is above all a servant of others, and he must continually work at being a sign pointing to Christ, a docile instrument in the Lord's hands. This is seen particularly in his humility in leading the liturgical assembly, in obedience to the rite, uniting himself to it in mind and heart, and avoiding anything that might give the impression of an inordinate emphasis on his own personality. I encourage the clergy always to see their eucharistic ministry as a humble service offered to Christ and his Church. The priesthood, as Saint Augustine said, is *amoris officium*, it is the office of the good shepherd, who offers his life for his sheep (cf. Jn 10:14-15).

Benedict XVI, Address of His Holiness to the Bishops of the United States, 16 April 2008:

Thus our devotion helps us to speak and act ***in persona Christi***, to teach, govern and sanctify the faithful in the name of Jesus, to bring his reconciliation, his healing and his love to all his beloved brothers and sisters. This radical configuration to Christ, the Good Shepherd, lies at the heart of our pastoral ministry, and if we open ourselves through prayer to the power of the Spirit, he will give us the gifts we need to carry out our daunting task, so that we need never "be anxious how to speak or what to say" (Mt 10:19).

In conclusion, then, the deacon does *not* act in or represent the person of Christ or the person of Christ the Head in any of his ministry. Rather, as introduced in BN for the Formation of Deacons [BN] (11), "he is constituted a living icon of Christ the servant within the Church [*icona vivens Christi servi in Ecclesia*]". To act in the person of Christ is not the same as being constituted an icon of Christ.

The International Theological Commission, who reviewed the history and contemporary state of the diaconate (as of 2003) noted that a change in Canon 1008 of the *CIC*, as Benedict XVI's *Motu Proprio* provided, was already envisioned prior to the publication of their "From the *Diakonia* of Christ to the *Diakonia* of the Apostles" (see its footnote no. 334, p. 124: "The International Theological Commission has been notified that a revised version of this canon is in preparation, aiming to distinguish the priestly ['*sacertotal*'] ministries from the diaconal ministry.")

This chapter may seem to belabor a point. The rationale is to convey an important conclusion: the Permanent Diaconate is a vocation distinct from the Priesthood. The deacon images Christ the Servant, while the priest acts in the person of Christ the Head. The three degrees of Orders are distinct yet interdependent. The diaconate has always been necessary, even when hidden beneath the chasuble. Since it is now much more visible, there is so much more for it to accomplish.

The deacon and his bishop

Directly or indirectly, the bishop of the diocese is involved in each man's diaconate formation as well as his diaconal ministry from the moment a man first applies to be considered for ordination. It is the bishop who appoints the director of formation and the director of the diaconate for his territory. The bishop approves the formation program, in all of its dimensions, and the defined components of each deacon's ministry in his designated parish or other assignment. Once a man enters formation, he is no longer a member of his home parish in the way he was before; rather he is now responsible to the director of formation as the representative of the bishop. This relationship continues throughout formation until ordination, at which point the deacon is responsible to the bishop through the director of deacons for the diocese.

If we remind ourselves of the circumstances that led the twelve apostles to appoint the Seven Hellenists, and the specific accounts of Stephen and Philip, we see that the spiritual power of the latter (the Seven) flowed through the former (the Twelve). In a like way, the *munera* of the deacon flows from the bishop. Accounts of the diaconate in the first few centuries of the Church emphasize the relationship with the episcopacy. The threefold ministry of each is hierarchical. Priest, prophet, and king are manifest in the bishop's role as high priest, *in persona Christi*, as the principal teacher of his flock, and as principal ruler, *in persona Christi Capitis*, of his diocese. The deacon proclaims the Word, serves at the altar, and ministers charity to the poor. (The priest exercises analogous responsibilities to the bishop within his parish.*)*

The regency of the bishop over his diocese is a pastoral authority. He has responsibility over the temporal goods of the local Church, and authority over his priests and deacons, to whom he delegates their own proper *munera*. Of course, both bishop and priest are responsible for lay and religious workers in their respective dioceses and parishes. The deacon has virtually no temporal authority intrinsic to his office. Rather, he ministers in his threefold manner, without attachment to any physical resources, except the limits of his parish and, to an extent, the diocese (some deacons may, in addition to their assigned ministry, serve as employees of parishes, dioceses, or other agency of the Church).

An ancient quote characterizes the deacon as the "eyes and ears of the bishop." Some deacons have interpreted this assertion as a special power, a kind of direct line to their ordinary. No, viewed in context, the deacon is entrusted with the power to deal with the everyday ministry that no one pastor could handle by himself. The bishop may be the principal teacher and regent of his territory, but it is his priests who celebrate the Eucharist and the sacraments of healing for the majority of the diocese, and it is deacons who are to be the herald of the Good News, calling the people to repentance, inviting them to the mercy of the Savior, and leading them to the altar of sacrifice.

The deacon's promise of obedience to the bishop, made at this ordination, imposes a serious obligation on both.

> Bishop: Do you promise respect and obedience to me and my successors?
>
> Candidates: I do.

By entrusting his ministry to the wisdom of the bishop, his promise of obedience has several dimensions, as implied by the meaning of the term. To be obedient is not merely and blindly carry out the superior's orders; it is to understand fully what is being asked of the deacon by his bishop. A key element of diaconal formation is training in following instructions, from simple to complex. And, then the would-be deacon is expected to be able to articulate (verbally and in writing) meaning and understanding. Should the man in formation not understand, he first needs to recognize that fact and then do everything in his power to rectify the problem, including dialog with his instructors and formators. When a bishop encourages his deacons to preach pro-life and pro-family homilies, the deacon should expect to be supported by his bishop and, one would hope, his pastor, should the deacon encounter opposition from an unorthodox parishioner. The bishop should also maintain open lines of communication, through his deacon director, so that the concerns of the deacons, especially as they relate to the people of the diocese, are met. The bishop, by having priests and deacons who are in obedience to him, has a special responsibility to see that he leads his clergy in right paths.

Most deacons are sent and assigned to parishes under the supervision of pastors. Effective ministry by the deacon, fulfilling the *munera* with which he is entrusted, should find himself in a strong supporting role to the parish priest in a manner similar to that by which he serves at the altar. It should be clear to every parishioner that the pastor is the final authority in the parish (as long as the pastor is fulfilling his own *munera*) and that the deacon's ministry, while distinct from the pastor, is collaborative and reinforcing. It is a special delight on the part of the bishop to know that he has parishes in which priests and deacons are working together to build up their little part of the Kingdom of God.

Two branches

With the restoration of the permanent diaconate, the ministry now once again has two branches and in a manner much more distinctive than in the early Church. The first branch of the diaconate, which is now the restored branch, is inferred to have originated in New Testament times; deacons, once called, maintained their ministry the rest of their life; however, in the West this ministry gradually faded away in the Early Church.

The second branch continues the trend that began in the early Middle Ages; men ordained to the diaconate were intended for eventual ordination to the ministerial priesthood and, for some, the episcopacy (ministry of bishop). In other words, for many centuries prior to Vatican II, ordination to the diaconate was rare unless it was to lead to the presbyterate. An example of one exception is St. Francis of Assisi, who preached often in church after church but refused priestly ordination.

Of course, transitional *diakonia* persists. Since 1970, then, men destined to be priests are still ordained to the diaconate first by essentially the same rite as those ordained to be permanent deacons. The only difference is the promise of celibacy that single men are required to make, whether they are intending to be priests or permanent deacons. (Married deacons understand that should their wife predecease them, they cannot remarry.)

The effects of ordination to the diaconate – the indelible character – and the faculties the newly ordained receive are the same for both transitional and permanent deacons. Further, the effects are retained even as the transitional deacon receives ordination to the priesthood and thereby receives the character of presbyter, as well as the additional *munera* and faculties proper to the priest.

Priests ordained prior to Vatican II may recount their diaconate as having lasted only a matter of days or weeks. They barely had time to consider the possibility that their souls had undergone an ontological change by virtue of their first ordination rite. It seems to have taken the clarity of Vatican Council II to illuminate the sacramental theology of all three degrees of Holy Orders (even the episcopacy was not clearly differentiated from the presbyterate prior to the Council). *LG* provided that clarity:

> Christ, whom the Father has sanctified and sent into the world, has through His apostles, made their successors, the bishops, partakers of His consecration and His mission. They have legitimately handed on to different individuals in the Church various degrees of participation in this ministry. Thus the divinely established ecclesiastical ministry is exercised on different levels by those who from antiquity have been called bishops, priests and deacons. Priests, although they do not possess the highest degree of the priesthood, and although they are dependent on the bishops in the exercise of their power, nevertheless they are united with the bishops in sacerdotal dignity. By the power of the sacrament of Orders, in the image of Christ the eternal high Priest, they are consecrated to preach the Gospel and shepherd the faithful and to celebrate divine worship, so that they are true priests of the New Testament. (*LG*28)

Among deacons who have reflected on the identity of priest and deacon, I have heard the hypothetical question, "Could not a priest be ordained without having been ordained a deacon first?" There are suggestions in Early Church history of deacons being ordained bishops, even Bishop of Rome, without clearly having been ordained priests first. However, it is not perfectly clear that either phenomenon, layman to priest, or deacon to bishop, skipping the intervening step, actually happened. If it did, one might infer that the indelible character of the deacon was itself imparted along with the indelible character of the presbyter in the first case, and the character of the presbyter along with the indelible episcopal character in the second.

The ontological change that happens with Baptism, Confirmation, and each degree of Orders is incompletely understood, beyond acquisition of the power, respectively, to be a Christian, to live fully the Christian life, and to exercise the received degree of clerical authority. As each character persists for all eternity, perhaps more mysteries are to be revealed in the life to come. In any case, as there is an association of each character with degrees of power and authority in this life, it is reasonable to assert that those *munera* received by the deacon upon his ordination continue to be exercised by priests and bishops out of their own diaconal ordination. In other words, presbyters baptize as both deacon and priest. The diaconal threefold ministry of Word, sacrament, and charity of the deacon, built upon his own baptism into the anointing of Christ, prophet, priest, and king, and his confirmation, is progressively overlain, by subsequent ordinations *in persona Christi Capitis*, to presbyter and bishop.

Should the preparation of transitional and permanent deacons for their intended vocation be the same? Of course, the answer has to be negative, if only because the transitional deacon is destined to the vocation of priest; his vocation is not to be a permanent deacon (although the character of his first ordination – to the diaconate is itself permanently retained). The secular (diocesan) priest is prepared not only for the administration of the sacraments, especially the Eucharist, Reconciliation, and Anointing of the Sick, but also for the pastoring of souls. The deacon cannot be a pastor or even a chaplain; the permanent deacon is not to be formed to be responsible for a parish or oratory, even though he might find himself administering either after ordination. His is the vocation of the threefold ministry of proclamation of the Word, service at the altar, and reaching out to the poor.

The shared ontological identity of transitional and permanent deacon continues, even as the former goes on to receive the additional character, *munera*, and faculty of presbyter. We can only conclude that the gift of the Spirit for strengthening for the ministry which is an essential of the ordination of the deacon is also necessary for the future priest: different formation, yes, but the same character, until the transitional deacon is enriched with the added character of the presbyter.

Why only men?

The "women's liberation" movement of the 1960s had several components, relaxation of sexual mores,   pursuit of equality in the workplace, and corollaries such as "no-fault" divorce, legalized and government-funded abortion, and free childcare. In recent years gay liberation/ marriage has been added to the agenda. While significant fulfillment of these nontraditional, − aspirations has been achieved, especially with the Supreme Court's 1973 Roe versus Wade decision, there remain many which have not been fully realized to the satisfaction of liberation advocates, even in states such as Massachusetts.

One additional manifestation of the liberation movement in the Catholic Church is the movement for ordination of women to the priesthood and, by necessity, then, the diaconate (both transitional and permanent). (Many non-Catholic denominations have admitted women into clerical leadership in recent decades.) The Catholic Magisterium has repeatedly emphasized that only men are validly ordained, as in Canon 1024:

> A baptized male alone receives sacred ordination validly. (*CIC*)

Further, the Catechism of the Catholic Church, after quoting Canon 1024, states:

> The Lord Jesus chose men (*viri*) to form the college of the twelve apostles, and the apostles did the same when they chose collaborators to succeed them in their ministry. The college of bishops, with whom the priests are united in the priesthood, makes the college of the twelve an ever-present and ever-active reality until Christ's return. The Church recognizes herself to be bound by this choice made by the Lord himself. For this reason the ordination of women is not possible. (Catechism of the Catholic Church, ¶1577)

The Catechism cites Scripture (Mark 3:14-19, Luke 6:12:16, 1 Timothy 3:1-13, 2 Timothy 1:6, Titus 1:5-9) and the early Church letter of St. Clement to the Corinthians; interestingly, the mention of appointed (ordained) men is almost an aside in (Pope) Clement's letter, within an admonishment to the Church of Corinth:

> And thus preaching through countries and cities, they [the apostles] appointed the first-fruits [of their labours], having first proved them by the Spirit, to be **bishops** and **deacons** of those who should afterwards believe. Nor was this any new thing, since indeed many ages before it was written concerning **bishops** and **deacons**. For thus says the Scripture a certain place, "I will appoint their **bishops** in righteousness, and their **deacons** in faith." ...
>
> We are of opinion, therefore, that those appointed by them [the apostles] , or afterwards by other eminent **men**, with the consent of the whole Church, and who have blamelessly served the flock of Christ in a humble, peaceable, and disinterested spirit, and have for a long time possessed the good opinion of all, cannot be justly dismissed from the ministry. ... But we see that you have removed some **men** of excellent behaviour from the ministry, which they fulfilled blamelessly and with honour. (Clement of Rome to the Corinthians, 42, 44)

Further, popes and Vatican congregations have emphasized the permanence and persistence of this teaching, that men only may be ordained to the priesthood, such as Paul VI, cited subsequently by John Paul II:

> When the question of the ordination of women arose in the Anglican Communion, Pope Paul VI, out of fidelity to his office of safeguarding the Apostolic Tradition, and also with a view to removing a new obstacle placed in the way of Christian unity, reminded Anglicans of the position of the Catholic Church [Paul VI, Response to the Letter of His Grace the Most Reverend Dr. F. D. Coggan, Archbishop of Canterbury, concerning the Ordination of Women to the Priesthood, November 30, 1975]:

74

She holds that it is not admissible to ordain women to the priesthood, for very fundamental reasons. These reasons include: the example recorded in the Sacred Scriptures of Christ choosing his Apostles only from among men; the constant practice of the Church, which has imitated Christ in choosing only men; and her living teaching authority which has consistently held that the exclusion of women from the priesthood is in accordance with God's plan for his Church. (Quoted by John Paul III, 1999, in *Ordinatio Sacerdotalis*).

Further, John Paul II writes, Paul VI directed the Congregation for the Doctrine of the Faith to set forth and expound the teaching of the Church on this matter. Their document, *Inter Insigniores*, stated:

[T]he Sacred Congregation for the Doctrine of the Faith judges it necessary to recall that the Church, in fidelity to the example of the Lord, does not consider herself authorized to admit women to priestly ordination. (Congregation for the Doctrine of the Faith, 1976, *Inter Insigniores*)

In defense of the solely male priesthood, *Inter Insigniores* cites Sacred Scripture, including all four Gospels and Acts, plus Paul's Letters to the Romans, Corinthians, Philippians, Thessalonians, Ephesians, and First Timothy. In addition, the writings of early Church Fathers, including Irenaeus, Tertullian, Firmilian of Caesarea, Cyprian, Origen, John Chrysostom, and Epiphanius are indicative, the document states, of a male-only priesthood. It furthers refers to works of the Scholastics, including Bonaventure, Richard of Middleton, John Duns Scotus, and Durandus of Saint Pourcain.

John Paul II concluded his Apostolic Letter with:

Wherefore, in order that all doubt may be removed regarding a matter of great importance, a matter which pertains to the Church's divine constitution itself, in virtue of my ministry of confirming the brethren (cf. Lk 22:32) I declare that the Church has no authority whatsoever to confer priestly ordination on women and that this judgment is to be definitively held by all the Church's faithful.

Most of the documents dealing with ordination of men emphasize the priesthood. However, what about the permanent diaconate, separately from the priesthood? As noted above, Canon Law states that only a man may receive ordination (implicitly referring to all three grades of Orders).

Most of the rationale of the documents discussed above focuses on the priesthood, especially its rootedness in the person of Christ and in the apostles whom he called to follow him. By analogy with the "example recorded in the Sacred Scriptures of Christ choosing his Apostles only from among men" (Paul VI), there are the seven upright men of Acts 7, traditionally viewed as proto-deacons, whom the apostles chose to minister to the Greek-speaking widows and orphans.

> At that time, as the number of disciples continued to grow, the Hellenists complained against the Hebrews because their widows were being neglected in the daily distribution. So the Twelve called together the community of the disciples and said, "It is not right for us to neglect the word of God to serve [διακονειν: diakonein] at table. Brothers, select from among you seven reputable **men**, filled with the Spirit and wisdom, whom we shall appoint to this task, whereas we shall devote ourselves to prayer and to the ministry of the word."
>
> The proposal was acceptable to the whole community, so they chose Stephen, a man filled with faith and the holy Spirit, also Philip, Prochorus, Nicanor, Timon, Parmenas, and Nicholas of Antioch, a convert to Judaism. They presented these men to the apostles who prayed and laid hands on them. (Acts 6:1-6; **emphasis** added)

Note that no women were selected to minister to the widows, but the seven men. The Ordination Rite of Deacons explicitly cites the Seven, along with the (male) Levites who ministered in the Temple, as examples for those to be ordained.

> You established a threefold ministry of worship and service for the glory of your name. As ministers of the tabernacle you chose the **sons** of Levi and gave them your blessing as their everlasting inheritance.
>
> In the first days of your Church under the inspiration of the Holy Spirit the apostles of your Son appointed seven **men** of good repute to assist them in the daily ministry, so that they themselves might be more free for prayer and preaching. By prayer and the laying on of the hands the apostles entrusted to those chosen men the ministry of serving at tables. (Ordination Rite of Deacons; **emphasis** added)

The Levites of the Hebrew Scriptures, who served in the tabernacle and in the temple, were males only. In the early Church of Rome, the deacons were referred to as Levites:

> Those, therefore, who present their offerings at the appointed times, are accepted and blessed; for inasmuch as they follow the laws of the Lord, they sin not. For his own peculiar services are assigned to the high priest, and their own proper place is prescribed to the priests, and their own special ministrations devolve on the **Levites**. The layman is bound by the laws that pertain to laymen. (Clement of Rome to the Corinthians, 40, **emphasis** added)

Also, there is one of the Scriptural examples of ordination of men alone cited in *Inter Insigniores* which is pertinent to deacons as well as priests:

> [T]he Apostle's forbidding of women "to speak" in the assemblies (cf. 1 Corinthians 14:34-35; 1 Timothy 2: 12) is of a different nature, and exegetes define its meaning in this way: Paul in no way opposes the right, which he elsewhere

recognizes as possessed by women, to prophesy in the assembly (cf. 1 Corinthians 11:5); the prohibition solely concerns the official function of teaching in the Christian assembly. For Saint Paul this prescription is bound up with the divine plan of creation (cf. 1 Corinthians 11:7; Genesis 2:18-24): it would be difficult to see in it the expression of a cultural fact. Nor should it be forgotten that we owe to Saint Paul one of the most vigorous texts in the New Testament on the fundamental equality of men and women, as children of God in Christ (cf. Galatians 3:28). (*Inter Insigniores* 4)

In the liturgy, the Gospel is assigned to the deacon, or in his absence, the priest. Further, only a priest, or on occasion, a deacon, may preach the homily. Only they, then, may preach and teach ("speak" in the Pauline sense) during worship.

What of the mention of women as deacons or deaconesses in Scripture and early Church? From what can be inferred, the ministry of such women was largely concerned with the instruction of women catechumens and accompanying them during baptism by the bishop as catechumens were unclothed during the Rite (FDC). It is not clear that any women designated as deacons or deaconesses ever exercised the ministry of the (male) deacon in the early Church.

Perhaps a pertinent distinction is that of efficacy or fruitfulness. 1131 of the Catechism:

> The sacraments are efficacious signs of grace, instituted by Christ and entrusted to the Church, by which divine life is dispensed to us. The visible rites by which the sacraments are celebrated signify and make present the graces proper to each sacrament. They bear fruit in those who receive them with the required dispositions.

Application of this distinction would imply that were the "ordained" ministry of women in the early Church fruitful and essential, and, therefore efficacious, it would still exist. I recall being asked some twenty years ago what I thought about the ordination of women to the priesthood in the Anglican Churches; I responded that perhaps we must see if their ministry proves fruitful. In any case as a non-Anglican and non-expert on Anglicanism I could say that such "ordinations" would be invalid and illicit in the Catholic Church in that they do not signify and accomplish all that is explicit and implied by Catholic Orders.

The diaconal ordination of men persisted in Roman Rite of the Catholic Church, even as it became largely a transitional ministry, hidden beneath and exercised through the priestly Order. The eventual recognition of the seven Sacraments at the Council of Trent emerged from the Church's reflection on their efficacy down through the ages. In a similar way, the early Church councils affirmed the fundamental Truths of the two natures of Christ – his humanity and divinity, the personhood of the Holy Spirit, and the Most Holy Trinity by reflection on Sacred Scripture and recognition of the fruits of the Gospel and the power of the Holy Spirit at work in those few Centuries since Pentecost.

Just as only a woman can be a mother of new human life and in the Spirit, and as the preeminent mother is Mary, *Theotokos*, the Christ-bearer, Mother of God, so only a man can be a father in the flesh and in the Spirit. The dignity of woman is equal to that of man. Their distinct humanity is complementary, both physically and spiritually.

> Husbands, love your wives, even as Christ loved the church and handed himself over for her. (Ephesians 5:25)

Even as Christ loves the Church, her dignity is affirmed; so too the love of the husband for his bride. And, the motherhood of the Virgin is elevated above even the hierarchy of the Church; she the mother of God raises the dignity of all mothers, indeed all faithful women, beyond all comprehension.

In 2001, three Vatican Congregations issued this statement:

Sept. 2001, Cardinals Joseph Ratzinger, Jorge Arturo Medina Estevez and Dario Castrillon Hoyos. The Notification was approved by the Pope on September 14.

1. Our offices have received from several countries signs of courses that are being planned or underway, directly or indirectly aimed at the diaconal ordination of women. Thus are born hopes which are lacking a solid doctrinal foundation and which can generate pastoral disorientation.

2. Since ecclesial ordination does not foresee such an ordination, it is not licit to enact initiatives which, in some way, aim to prepare candidates for diaconal ordination.

3. The authentic promotion of women in the Church, in conformity with the constant ecclesial Magisterium, with special reference to (the Magisterium) of His Holiness John Paul II, opens other ample prospectives of service and collaboration.

4. The undersigned Congregations—within the sphere of their proper authority—thus turn to the individual ordinaries, asking them to explain (this) to their own faithful and to diligently apply the above-mentioned directives. (Notification on the Diaconal Ordination of Women, Congregations for Doctrine of Faith, for Worship and Discipline of Sacraments, and for Clergy, September 17, 2001)

The International Theological Commission studied the distinction between the ordained deacon and the ministry of the deaconess in the early Church (From the *Diakonia* of Christ to the *Diakonia* of the Apostles, 2003) and subsequently offered a clarification of the results of their research:

The general secretary of the International Theological Commission, Father Georges Cottier, O. P., has responded to certain questions about the Commission's study of the diaconate raised by the October 8th [2002] issue of La Croix.

Fr. Cottier stated that the Commission's study has not concluded that the possibility that women could be ordained to the diaconate remains open, as asserted by La Croix, but rather tends to support the exclusion of this possibility.

The Commission of theologians, even if it has not the role of pronouncing with the authority, which is characteristic of the Magisterium, presented two important indications which emerge from study of the matter. In the first place, the Commission observed that the deaconesses mentioned in the tradition of the early Church cannot simply be assimilated to ordained deacons. In support of this conclusion, Fr. Cottier noted that both the rite of institution and the functions exercised by deaconesses distinguished them from ordained deacons.

Furthermore, Fr. Cottier noted that the Commission's study reaffirmed the unity of the sacrament of Holy Orders. The distinction between the ministry of bishops and priests, on the one hand, and that of deacons, on the other hand, is nonetheless embraced within the unity of the sacrament of Holy Orders. The Commission's reaffirmation of this teaching arose from a careful study of the ecclesial tradition, of the documents of the Second Vatican Council, and of the post conciliar Magisterium of the Church.

Fr. Cottier stated that "it belongs to the Magisterium to pronounce with authority on the question, taking into account the historical and theological research presented by the study of the International Theological Commission."

The International Theological Commission devoted over five years of research to the topic of the history and theology of the diaconate before approving the text of its study at its recently concluded meeting. The study was produced at the request of the Congregation for the Doctrine of the Faith. (Zenit, October 30, 2002, http://www.zenit.org/en/articles/theological-commission-s-statement-on-women-s-ordination-to-diaconate.)

At present, then, there seems to be no basis for assuming that future ordination of women to the diaconate is likely to occur. Some have parsed translations of dialogs with Pope Francis to imply such an action might be forthcoming, but no official Church pronouncement has been made along such lines.

Because this chapter deals with the intrinsic maleness of ordained ministry, it reads, perhaps, as an insensitive proof-text. And, perhaps John Paul II recognized that the seemingly dry defense of Tradition always needs the recognition of complementarity of the sexes. In any case he provided a novel letter to women, with a litany of "thank-you's" regarding the tangible and intangible "genius of women":

Thank you, *women who are mothers!*

Thank you, *women who are wives!*

Thank you, *women who are daughters* and *women who are sisters!*

Thank you, *consecrated women!*

Thank you, *every woman,* for the simple fact of being *a woman!* (Letter of John Paul II to Women, June 29, 1995, http://www.vatican.va/holy_father/john_paul_ii/letters/documents/hf_jp-ii_let_29061995_women_en.html)

The Pauline foundation of the Sacrament of Matrimony

(Adapted from "Ephesians 5: Bridegroom and Bride," originally published in Homiletic and Pastoral Review, July, 2009, http://www. hprweb. com/2009/07/ephesians-5-bridegroom-and-bride/)

> By submitting herself to her husband, the wife is allowing her man to sacrifice himself for her.

It is Mass on the Twenty-first Sunday of Ordinary Time, in late summer some years ago. Fortunately the air conditioning seems to be holding up, for this year at least. The celebrant offers the Opening Prayer, asking the Father for help, to seek the values that will bring lasting joy in a changing world. Seated beside the celebrant, the deacon at this Mass, I join the assembly in preparing to listen to the Word of God. The Scripture readings are from Year B, and we hear the stirring invitation of Joshua: "Decide today whom you will serve ... As for me and my household, we will serve the Lord" (Josh. 24:15). The cantor leads us to respond: "Taste and see the goodness of the Lord."

But next comes the one passage that no one really seems (or wants) to listen to; out of all of Scripture proclaimed over the complete three-year cycle, this is one passage that is consistently ignored, rejected, or misinterpreted – I call it the "nudging" Scripture. After twenty-plus years of ordained ministry, sitting in the sanctuary behind the ambo, every third year I can watch for the elbows. The reader begins:

> A reading from the Letter of St. Paul to the Ephesians.
>
> Brothers and sisters, be subordinate to one another out of reverence for Christ.

Show humility and defer to others, as we often hear in other readings, but are we ready for the next sentence?

> Wives should be subordinate to their husbands as to the Lord.

Suddenly, the many male faces are alert; the wives of the quickest feel an elbow against their arms. And the faces of some women fall, eyes cast down; it is as if their minds can read: "Oh, no. Not again. Not this Sunday." (In fairness, some women raise their heads, as if to indicate that they indeed like the Scripture – maybe they have heard me preach on it before.)

> For the husband is head of his wife...

More nudges and smirks creep across male faces. However, in the self-satisfaction of men and the embarrassment, even indignation of the women, the remaining phrases of the current sentence are missed:

> ...just as Christ is head of the Church, he himself the savior of the body.

A seemingly three-fold admonition is fulfilled with the next sentence:

> As the Church is subordinate to Christ, so wives should be subordinate to their husbands in everything.

The "triumph" of the husband on this hot summer day contrasts with the flushed cheeks, embarrassment, perhaps even anger, of too many wives. And, the remainder of the passage remains unheard and unheralded:

> Husbands, love your wives, even as Christ loved the Church and handed himself over for her to sanctify her, cleansing her by the bath of water with the word, that he might present to himself the Church in splendor, without spot or wrinkle or any such thing, that she might be holy and without blemish.

> So (also) husbands should love their wives as their own bodies. He who loves his wife loves himself. For no one hates his own flesh but rather nourishes and cherishes it, even as Christ does the Church, because we are members of his body. For this reason a man shall leave (his) father and

(his) mother and be joined to his wife, and the two shall become one flesh.

This is a great mystery, but I speak in reference to Christ and the Church.

In anticipation of this passage, whether from previous liturgies over the years, or in conscious awareness of the so–called women's movement in the larger culture, the assigned homilist for that Sunday in the three year cycle may decide to either ignore the second reading entirely or have the reader proclaim the "shorter" version, thereby leaving out the "offending" submission and headship phrases. Worse, so I have been told (but never observed), different passages are substituted or, worst of all, the wording of the text changed.

The irony of this situation is that Ephesians 5:21-33 is a critical passage for the self-understanding of the Church, the nature of the sacraments of Matrimony and Holy Orders, and the theology of the body (there is two-fold meaning in this latter term), both human and divinized. Ephesians 5 is a two-way lens through which other critical passages of Scripture are illuminated and magnified. Human limitation necessitates that the Word be heard in fragments, Sunday after Sunday, but Catholic understanding of Scripture requires that it be understood whole and complete.

First, let us deal with the glaring issue of "submission." If all we were to read or hear were these three fragments, "Wives should be subordinate to their husbands as to the Lord... For the husband is the head of his wife...wives should be subordinate to their husbands in everything," we would not be able to engage in Catholic understanding. Not only must we consider the entire passage, we need to consider the entire Pauline corpus, reflect on the four Gospels, and, ultimately, take all of Divine Revelation into account. Why? Because "This is a great mystery, but I speak in reference to Christ and the Church."

What is the nature of the submission called for? "...subordinate...as to the Lord." Is the husband taking the place of Christ? Seemingly so: "As the Church is subordinate to Christ…" But what might this mean?

Look at what is required of the husband: "Husbands, love your wives, even as Christ loved the Church…" How did Christ love the Church? He "handed himself over for her." Christ Jesus sacrificed himself for her, the Church. Is not sacrifice of oneself unto death for another the ultimate submission, the complete subordination? Recall how the passage begins: "Be subordinate to one another."

By submitting herself to her husband, the wife is allowing her man to sacrifice himself for her! More critically, the very nature of human procreation requires initiation and culmination of the intimate bond by the male, as the two become one flesh (Gen. 2:24), as an expression of natural love, *eros*:

> First, *eros* is somehow rooted in man's very nature; Adam is a seeker, who "abandons his mother and father" in order to find woman; only together do the two represent complete humanity and become "one flesh." The second aspect is equally important. From the standpoint of creation, *eros* directs man towards marriage, to a bond which is unique and definitive; thus, and only thus, does it fulfill its deepest purpose. Corresponding to the image of a monotheistic God is monogamous marriage. marriage based on exclusive and definitive love becomes the icon of the relationship between God and his people and vice versa. God's way of loving becomes the measure of human love. This close connection between *eros* and marriage in the Bible has practically no equivalent in extra-biblical literature (*Deus Caritas Est*).

We encounter in Ephesians 5 a profound analogy, which, illuminating the mystery of the relationship between Christ and the Church, contemporaneously unveils the essential truth about marriage: that is, that

> marriage corresponds to the vocation of Christians only when it reflects the love which Christ the Bridegroom gives to the Church, His Bride, and which the Church (resembling

the "subject" wife, that is, completely given) attempts to return to Christ (John Paul II, 1986, The Theology of marriage and Celibacy, St. Paul Editions, p. 194).

For the Christian husband and wife are themselves part of the Church, "members of his body," the Bride of Christ. Within the body of Christ (initiated by Christ's sacrifice), the husband submits to Christ as a member of his body, sacrifices himself for his wife, who subordinates herself to both him and Christ by accepting her husband's sacrifice. As John Paul II further wrote:

> ...the first subject, Christ, manifests the love with which He has loved her [the Church] by giving himself for her. That love is an image and above all a model of the love which the husband should show to his wife in marriage, when the two are subject to one another "out of reverence for Christ" (Theology of marriage and Celibacy, p. 202).

New members of the Church are begotten as husband and wife become one and bring their children to "the bath of water with the word." (Ephesians 5:11)

The sacramentality of marriage is, then, a further enfleshment of the sacrifice of Christ for the Church manifested in the sacrifice of the husband for his bride. The birth of the Church and her marriage to Christ occurred simultaneously on the Cross, as water and blood poured forth from his side (John 19:34), and was foreshadowed at Cana (John 2:1-10). Christ becomes one flesh with the Church each time Eucharist is celebrated and received.

Ephesians 5, illuminating the rest of Sacred Scripture, compels us to accept and assert those fundamental teachings of the Church that are under attack today.

- Each marriage consists of one man and one woman.
- The man is husband; the woman is wife. (i. e., there is no gender confusion)
- marriage lasts until death (for they are one flesh).
- The Church has one Savior, one Bridegroom.

- Sacramental marriage is not only the image of Christ's love for the Church, it accomplishes that love.
- The minister of the Eucharist is male, acting *in persona Christi*.

So what should the homilist on the Twenty-first Sunday of Year B preach? Proclaim the mystery! The Christian mystery is neither hidden nor waiting to be deduced; it is revealed in the Gospel, the witness of the Church, and in the living out of the sacraments, and awaits fulfillment in the second coming of the Bridegroom. Provide the opportunity for each married woman in the assembly to recognize or be reminded of her dignity as a wife, the image of the Bride of Christ. Challenge all husbands to accept and fulfill their image of the Bridegroom who sacrifices himself for his Bride, the Church, thereby in their sacrifice, to make their wives ever more worthy of Christ. Give the unmarried a vision of their dignity within the Body as Bride of Christ. As the Gospel of that Sunday states (and I as Deacon am honored to proclaim):

Simon Peter answered him, "Master, to whom shall we go? You have the words of eternal life. We have come to believe and are convinced that you are the Holy One of God" (John 6:68-69).

The married deacon

Let us speculate a bit about the action of the Spirit in the Church beginning with Vatican Council II and extending into the present day. *Lumen Gentium* and *Ad Gentes* both called for a restoration of the permanent diaconate in the Western Church, including bestowal of ordination on married candidates. In a practical sense, it is the *married* diaconate that was restored by the Council. The possibility of celibate permanent deacons was very real, even though rare, in the Church prior to Vatican II. This possibility, however, was rarely realized simply because most men called to celibacy by the Spirit heard the larger call to the priesthood, not to a permanent diaconate; alternatively, many men called to celibacy heard it as part of a call to the religious life as a vowed brother or monk. The exceptional example which exemplifies the rule is St. Francis of Assisi. There appears to be no doubt that Francis could have been ordained to the priesthood, but declined, and thereby ministered as a deacon, preaching in church after church, while building the Order of Friars Minor. It is fair to suggest, I think, that the need for priests has overshadowed the ordinary ministry of the (celibate) deacon through much of the Church's history. Rather, the ministry itself was exercised (1) sacramentally, through the priesthood, as if the otherwise visible *diakonia* were overlain by the chasuble, and (2) charismatically, through the ministry of vowed religious in monasteries and the charitable orders.

In order to restore the diaconate in the numbers desired (after ancient Rome, seven per parish?) to penetrate the larger society, it only made sense to consider inviting married men to formation and ordination. Why not include perpetual continence as a prerequisite to ordination of married men? In fact, there have been cases of married couples making promises of continence ("Josephite" marriages), which, with explicit approval from Rome further allow for the husband to receive Orders (almost always presbyterate) and the wife to either enter a religious order or live alone. So, even this opportunity already existed prior to Vatican II.

What is distinctive about the restoration of the diaconate is the possibility of ordained married men who stay married in every sense of the state. As indicated by the Directory of Ministry and Life of the Deacon, the state of a deacon, whether celibate or married, is to enrich both his ministry and his spirituality. For the celibate, he is to draw upon his baptism, confirmation, and ordination, supported by Eucharist and Reconciliation, and the gift of celibacy itself. The married deacon is to draw upon all of the same sacraments *plus his marriage* to enrich his relationship with those whom he serves thereby fulfilling the objectives of all of the sacraments.

I have not mentioned another aspect of ordained ministry of a married man – the ordination of former Anglican priests and Lutheran ministers who have been received into the Catholic Church. No matter where one falls on the question of married priests in the Western Church, I suspect that the ordination of married deacons is essentially irrelevant to a married Roman Rite presbyterate comparable to that of the Eastern Rite Churches.

Permanent deacons are not priests, nor are they necessarily destined for the priesthood; and, doctrinally, they do not share in the ministerial priesthood. Yes, only deacons can be ordained to the priesthood; however, the restored permanent diaconate is not intended to form men for priesthood, but for the distinct ministry of the deacon. Under normal conditions, transitional deacons who are ordained to the priesthood have been explicitly formed for the priesthood, not the diaconate.

As noted above, the distinction between transitional and permanent deacons is canonically and practically real, even if the sacramental *effects* of diaconal ordination are identical. Formation-preparation for ministry – is not nor should it necessarily be the same for priestly and permanent diaconal ministry. The months that a young man spends as a deacon prior to his priestly ordination may involve much of what is diaconal ministry, except for the ministry of a married deacon to his wife and family (the latter's primary ministry, after all); however, the transitional deacon's orientation is still forward-looking, to that time in which he is to celebrate Mass, offer absolution, administer the sacrament of the sick, and, finally, pastor a flock, as well as administering the same rites as he did as a deacon.

The ministry of the permanent deacon is upon ordination, immediate, in Word, Sacrament, and Charity and for years to come, not next year alone. That Rome has provided an accommodation for the ordination to the priesthood of married ministers in other sacramental communions is remarkable and welcoming to them and the community that joins with them; however, it is not relevant to the ministry of the married deacons, beyond the obvious possibility that married deacons and married former Anglican priests or Lutheran ministers might serve together, and would thereby share in the commonalities of ministers with a married home life.

I suggest, then, that the married diaconate, in the fullness of both sacraments, is the essential new gift that Vatican Council II offers the Church in the restoration of the ministry; however, the new gift draws from the ancient tradition witnessed in the late and immediately post-Apostolic era. It is not the harbinger of a future, normative married priesthood. The added celibate diaconate vocations (in addition to widowed deacons) that have accompanied the married diaconate since the restoration are welcome *lagniappe* (bonuses).

I believe that the Spirit is moving, even compelling the witness of the ordained minister – the deacon (both the celibate and married) – as well as the lay apostolate into the world outside of the visible Church.

What does Church law require?

Canon Law of the Catholic Church (*CIC*) delineates prerequisites for a man to be considered for ordination to the diaconate. Even prior to this, of course, the permanent diaconate must actually exist within a country and diocese. It is for the Episcopal Conference to decide whether to ask permission of the Holy See to implement the permanent diaconate and for the individual bishop to opt for the restoration of the permanent diaconate in his diocese. Thus, the existence of the permanent diaconate in a diocese provides the basis for consideration of men for eventual ordination.

The prerequisites for a man destined for ordination to the permanent diaconate include having received the sacraments of initiation (Baptism, Confirmation, Eucharist), completion of a designated formation program, and age 35 or older (married candidates) or 25 or older (celibate candidates). Episcopal Conferences have the competence to increase the required age for ordination and provide norms for formation. Married candidates must also have the permission of their wives.

Ordination must be a free request of the candidate; he cannot be compelled to receive ordination. Neither can the candidate's desire compel the Church to ordain him. Both desires must be present. The bishop (or superior of a religious order) is responsible for appropriate instruction, and, with all circumstances addressed, makes the prudent judgment that only those are to receive orders who

> ... have integral faith, are moved by the right intention, have the requisite knowledge, possess a good reputation, and are endowed with integral morals and proven virtues and the other physical and psychic qualities in keeping with the order to be received (*CIC*, Canon 1029)

Canon Law of the Catholic Church provides several distinct, normative conditions which preclude a man from receiving Orders. Such a defined condition – an "impediment" – includes psychological illness which precludes fulfillment of the ordained ministry; engaging in apostasy, heresy, or schism; an attempt at invalid marriage; participation in murder or abortion; mutilation of self or another; or acting as a priest or bishop in whole or in part. A married Catholic man can be considered for ordination to the diaconate, but not to higher orders; an unmarried man can be considered for either eventual priestly or permanent diaconal ordination. The occupation of a man must not be contrary to Church teaching, and one who is recently received into the Church must wait for ordination for as long as the particular law of his diocese provides.

> The decision to undertake the path of diaconal formation can come about either upon the initiative of the aspirant himself or by means of an explicit proposal of the community to which the aspirant belongs. In each case, the decision must be accepted and shared by the community. (BN, 40)

After meeting the prerequisites for consideration for eventual ordination, the man and representatives of the Church engage in a period of formation which involves two components: (1) growth of the man in intellectual knowledge, human character, practical experience, pastoral sensibility, and, especially, intimacy with the Triune God and (2) discernment by the man and those responsible for his formation as to the existence of a clear, concrete call to the diaconate. BN declares:

> ... This discernment must be conducted on the basis of objective criteria, which treasure the ancient tradition of the Church and take account of present day pastoral needs. For the discernment of vocations to the permanent diaconate, some requirements of a general nature and others responding to the particular state of life of those called should be taken into account. (BN, 29)

Church Law rests on Sacred Scripture and Tradition. As BN notes:

> The first diaconal profile was outlined in the First Letter of Saint Paul to Timothy: "Deacons likewise must be serious,

not double-tongued, not addicted to much wine, not greedy for gain; they must hold the mystery of the faith with a clear conscience. And let them also be tested first; then if they prove themselves blameless let them serve as deacons... Let deacons be the husband of one wife, and let them manage their children and their households well; for those who serve well as deacons gain a good standing for themselves and also great confidence in the faith which is in Jesus Christ" (*1 Timothy* 3:8-10. 12-13).

The qualities listed by Paul are prevalently human, almost as if to say that deacons could carry out their ministry only if they were acceptable models of humanity. We find echoes of Paul's exhortation in texts of the Apostolic Fathers, especially in the *Didachè* and Saint Polycarp. The *Didachè* urges: "Elect for yourselves therefore bishops and deacons worthy of the Lord, meek men, not lovers of money, honest and proven," and Saint Polycarp counsels: "In like manner should the deacons be blameless before the face of his righteousness, as being the servants of God and Christ, and not of men. They must not be slanderers, double-tongued, or lovers of money, but temperate in all things, compassionate, industrious, walking according to the truth of the Lord, who was the servant of all." (BN, 30)

In the early Church, its experience with leadership gradually shaped the meaning of the diaconate, presbyterate, and episcopacy.

The Church's tradition subsequently finalised and refined the requirements which support the authenticity of a call to the diaconate. These are firstly those which are valid for orders in general [Canon 1029, as above, is then quoted]. . . . . (BN, 31)

Both natural and infused characteristics are pertinent as objects for evaluation of potential candidates.

The profile of candidates is then completed with certain specific human qualities and evangelical virtues necessary for *diakonia*. Among the human qualities which should be highlighted are: psychological maturity, capacity for dialogue and communication, sense of responsibility, industriousness, equilibrium and prudence. Particularly important among the evangelical virtues: prayer, Eucharistic and Marian devotion, a humble and strong *sense of the Church*, love for the Church and her mission, spirit of poverty, capacity for obedience and fraternal communion, apostolic zeal, openness to service, charity towards the brothers and sisters. (BN, 32)

The candidate's active service in his parish and in the larger community should manifest his natural and gifted experience.

In addition, candidates for the diaconate must be active members of a Christian community and already have exercised praiseworthy commitment to the apostolate. (BN, 33)

Perhaps one of the more extraordinary facets of the permanent diaconate is the diversity of origins each has.

They may come from every social grouping and carry out any work or professional activity, providing that it is not, according to the norms of the Church and the prudent judgement of the Bishop, inconsistent with the diaconal state. (37) Furthermore, such activity must be compatible in practice with commitments of formation and the effective exercise of the ministry. (BN, 34)

The deacon and liturgy

Deacons often find themselves in awkward positions when it comes to exercising their liturgical roles. Since the first ordinations after the restoration of the permanent diaconate, the function of the deacon, especially at Mass, has seemed at times difficult and/or confusing to deacons, if not ambiguous. In part the difficulties involved the degrees to which those responsible for the liturgy (usually the pastor, but not always) took the diaconal role into account. Veteran deacons from the Seventies and early Eighties can each relate their own experiences along these lines.

Having been ordained in 1988, I have now served in six parishes in three different dioceses. While I could recount my own liturgical experiences (and those of fellow deacons who have related theirs to me), I'm not sure that there would be much edification in the effort. Part of the diversity of experience in the first few decades of the restored diaconate was *apparent* ambiguity in the liturgical documents, and, more important, incomplete implementation of the directives. Presently, the worshipping Church, including deacons, has a much clearer roadmap for serving the celebration of the Sacrifice. This roadmap is provided by the revised General Instruction to the (Third) Roman Missal (*IGMR*), originally translated into English for the United States in 2002, the juridical instruction, *Redemptionis Sacramentum* in 2004 (RS), and, especially (in English-speaking countries) the new translation of the Third Edition of the Roman Missal, including the slightly revised *IGMR* (introduced in the United States in 2011).

Unfortunately, some of those deacons who have been ordained for some years may have acquired attitudes toward their service of the liturgy and relationship to the celebrant and other ministers that might inhibit acceptance, if not the whole—hearted embrace of the changes provided by the *IGMR*, the full Missal, and directives of *RS*. Perhaps they have not been open to change to the degree they should be. Catholics – especially Catholic ministers – need to be open to continuous conversion and change. The even greater challenge comes when Catholics – again, especially the ministers – are called to be the prophets of such change. Further, for those considering the ministry of deacon, a willingness to learn and adapt to the preferred, even essential, instructions of the liturgy is not optional. Imitation of non–conformable practice of more experienced deacons is to be avoided. Men entering formation to become deacons are often confronted with liturgical practices different from that of their home parishes.

What should guide attitudes towards changes in the liturgy? As noted above, BN states that the deacon is to be a *"living icon of Christ the servant within the Church"* (paragraph 11). There is a dignity to the ministry of the deacon ("service of the servant"), and that dignity is especially expressed liturgically in proper, conscientious service of the altar.

What are the changes that directly, or even indirectly, involve the deacon? *RS*, which was produced by the Congregation for the Divine Worship at the prompting of St. Pope John Paul II, enumerates a number of items that may have been incompletely implemented by parishes in response to the initially translated revised General Instruction to the Roman Missal. Several of the changes involve deacons.

The rest of this chapter is written from the perspective of deacon to deacon. Prospective deacons can read the text by imagining what it might be to be a minister at the altar?

Deacons are addressed directly by *RS* (**emphasis** added by author):

> Let all **Deacons**, then, do their part so that the Sacred Liturgy will be celebrated according to the norms of the duly approved liturgical books. (*RS*, 35)

Deacons may need to be the catalyst of change, humbly urging pastors to consider what the revised liturgy requires. Let's consider those aspects of RS and the *IGMR* that directly concern deacons and that may not be completely implemented.

a) When he is present at the celebration of the Eucharist, a **Deacon** should exercise his ministry, wearing sacred vestments. In fact, the Deacon:assists the Priest and walks at his side;

b) ministers at the altar, both as regards the chalice and the book;

c) proclaims the Gospel and may, at the direction of the Priest Celebrant, give the Homily (cf. no. 66);

d) guides the faithful people by giving appropriate instructions, and announces the intentions of the Universal Prayer;

e) assists the Priest Celebrant in distributing Communion, and purifies and arranges the sacred vessels;

f) carries out the duties of other ministers himself, if necessary, when none of them is present. . (*IGMR* 171)

Consider the principal aspects of the Mass that involve the deacon:

Liturgical Vesture

Alb

"The alb" [the white liturgical garment which is foundational for all three degrees of Holy Orders, and which is designed to cover the street or clerical wear; lay ministers may also wear it according to parochial custom]is "to be tied at the waist with a cincture unless it is made so as to fit even without a cincture. Before the alb is put on, if it does not completely cover the ordinary clothing at the neck, an amice should be put on." (*RS*, 122)

For whatever reasons, many deacons (and priests!) may incorrectly omit the cincture with albs that do not have a built–in belt.

Dalmatic

The proper vestment of the **Deacon** is the dalmatic, to be worn over an alb and stole. In order that the beautiful tradition of the Church may be preserved, it is praiseworthy to refrain from exercising the option of omitting the dalmatic. (*RS*, 125)

Deacons are strongly encouraged to wear the dalmatic.

Vessels and Preparation of Gifts

... [t]he pouring of the Blood of Christ after the consecration from one vessel to another is completely to be avoided, lest anything should happen that would be to the detriment of so great a mystery... (*RS*, 106)

Fulfilling this instruction requires special thought. Some parishes can have chalices, already filled with wine, brought to the altar during the preparation of gifts. Other parishes, especially those with steps up or down into the sanctuary, may prefer a flagon of wine, presented with the gifts and poured into chalices during the preparation. The deacon can facilitate the choice as Ordinary Minister of the chalice.

Texts of the Liturgy

The reprobated practice by which Priests, **Deacons** or the faithful here and there alter or vary at will the texts of the Sacred Liturgy that they are charged to pronounce, must cease. For in doing thus, they render the celebration of the Sacred Liturgy unstable, and not infrequently distort the authentic meaning of the Liturgy. (*RS*, 59)

For the deacon the new English version of the Missal provides some freedom in places, especially the third form of the Penitential Act, and not in others. *"Let us offer each other the sign of peace,"* does not provide freedom to alter its form. Similarly, there are four distinct dismissal formulae, but no permission to modify them:

Go forth, the Mass is ended.

Go and announce the Gospel of the Lord.

Go in peace, glorifying God by your life.

Go in peace.

Neither lay person nor cleric may change *licitly* the texts of Sacred Scripture or the Liturgy, especially in the substitution of pronouns, or the deletion of verses (consider, for example, Ephesians 5). The temptation to make either the Sign of Peace or the Dismissal a mini–homily is not provided for in the Missal or the General Instruction.

Book of the Gospels

> Carrying the Book of the Gospels slightly elevated, the **Deacon** precedes the Priest as he approaches the altar or else walks at the Priest's side. (*IGMR* 172)

Unless a parish cannot afford it, there should be a Book of the Gospels. If a deacon is absent or unable to carry the book, a layperson may carry it. The book is carried in procession at the beginning of Mass, but not at the end.

Homily

The homily, which is given in the course of the celebration of Holy Mass and is a part of the Liturgy itself,

> "should ordinarily be given by the Priest celebrant himself. He may entrust it to a concelebrating Priest or occasionally, according to circumstances, to a **Deacon**, but never to a layperson…" (*RS*, 64)

The homily is not the deacon's by right, but by faculty and delegation.

Prayer of the Faithful

> After the introduction by the Priest, it is the **Deacon** himself who announces the intentions of the Universal Prayer, usually from the ambo. (*IGMR* 177)

Particularly when he enters a parish which previously has not had a deacon, fulfillment of this instruction requires some delicacy, as the Prayer is read by a lay person in the absence of a deacon. Yet, the distinct identity of the deacon is expressed in this function.

Preparation of Gifts

After the Universal Prayer, while the Priest remains at the chair, the **Deacon** prepares the altar, assisted by the acolyte, but it is the **Deacon's** place to take care of the sacred vessels himself. He also assists the Priest in receiving the people's gifts. After this, he hands the Priest the paten with the bread to be consecrated, pours wine and a little water into the chalice, saying quietly, By the mystery of this water, etc., and after this presents the chalice to the Priest. He may also carry out the preparation of the chalice at the credence table. If incense is being used, the Deacon assists the Priest during the incensation of the offerings, the cross, and the altar; and after this the Deacon himself or the acolyte incenses the Priest and the people. (*IGMR* 178)

Note the subtlety of handing the paten and the chalice to the priest (not placing them on the corporal). And, the use of incense is normative. Liturgy committees may want to reflect upon the implications of using incense more frequently. Ideally there should be four altar servers when incense is used: thurifer (thurible and incense-bearer), cross–bearer, and two torchbearers.

Eucharistic Prayer

The proclamation of the Eucharistic Prayer, which by its very nature is the climax of the whole celebration, is proper to the Priest by virtue of his Ordination. It is therefore an abuse … to proffer it in such a way that some parts of the Eucharistic Prayer are recited by a **Deacon**, a lay minister, or by an individual member of the faithful, or by all members of the faithful together. The Eucharistic Prayer, then, is to be recited by the Priest alone in full. (*RS*, 52)

Early in the ministry of the restored diaconate, in many dioceses and/or parishes, the *Mysterium Fidei* had been introduced by the deacon ("Let us proclaim the mystery of faith", now simply "The mystery of faith") while not so indicated in the Missal. Because it is not so indicated, its enunciation is proper to the main priest–celebrant alone.

> During the Eucharistic Prayer, the **Deacon** stands near the Priest, but slightly behind him, so that when necessary he may assist the Priest with the chalice or the Missal.

> From the epiclesis until the Priest shows the chalice, the **Deacon** usually remains kneeling. If several **Deacons** are present, one of them may place incense in the thurible for the Consecration and incense the host and the chalice at the elevation. (*IGMR* 179)

The deacon does not kneel until the *epiclesis* (the invocation of the Holy Spirit over the gifts; note that within Eucharistic Prayer I – the Roman Canon – blessing of the gifts occurs prior to the epiclesis). While kneeling, bowing the head when the celebrant genuflects is *not* indicated. (Deacons who are unable to kneel remain standing and bow after the elevations of the host and the chalice.) The deacon rises after the elevation of the chalice (prior to the *Mysterium Fidei*) – rising as the celebrant rises (after the priest's second genuflection following the words of institution over the chalice). [A personal observation: The ordination of the deacon occurs with an epiclesis by the bishop while the candidate is kneeling. We knelt in the presence of the person of Christ in the bishop as he ordained us and we kneel in the presence of the person of Christ in the priest as he offers the words of institution.]

> At the concluding doxology of the Eucharistic Prayer, the Deacon stands next to the Priest, and holds the chalice elevated while the Priest elevates the paten with the host, until the people have acclaimed, Amen. (*IGMR* 180)

The deacon follows the action of the celebrant – as the priest lowers the paten, the deacon lowers the chalice. (Some priests may not wait until the Amen is completed.)

Sign of Peace

> After the Priest has said the prayer for the Rite of Peace and the greeting The peace of the Lord be with you always and the people have replied, And with your spirit, the **Deacon**, if appropriate, says the invitation to the Sign of Peace. With hands joined, he faces the people and says, Let us offer each other the sign of peace. Then he himself receives the Sign of Peace from the Priest and may offer it to those other ministers who are nearest to him. (*IGMR* 181)

Notice that no gesture is to accompany the invitation. The Sign of Peace can become prolonged and undignified; again, the deacon may not be in a position to maintain its dignity, but he can try to limit the indignity.

Breaking of Bread

> In the celebration of Holy Mass the breaking of the Eucharistic Bread—done only by the Priest celebrant, if necessary with the help of a **Deacon** or of a concelebrant— begins after the exchange of peace, while the *Agnus Dei* is being recited …. the Rite must be carried out with great reverence. Even so, it should be brief. The abuse that has prevailed in some places, by which this Rite is unnecessarily prolonged and given undue emphasis, with laypersons also helping in contradiction to the norms, should be corrected with all haste. (*RS*, 73)

We encounter here another of the larger challenges of the new instructions – limitations on the role of lay people in the liturgy – in this case extraordinary ministers of Holy Communion (via a temporary dispensation, extraordinary ministers in the United States assisted with the distribution of consecrated hosts into additional ciboria, pouring of the Precious Blood and, purification of vessels after Communion. However this permission expired without renewal). And, liturgists and musicians may be involved in any changes also; with the Precious Blood no longer being poured into the chalices, there is no longer need for extra verses of the *Agnus Dei*, which are not provided in any case.

Communion

> After the Priest's Communion, the **Deacon** receives Communion under both kinds from the Priest himself and then assists the Priest in distributing Communion to the people. If Communion is given under both kinds, the Deacon himself administers the chalice to the communicants; and, when the distribution is over, standing at the altar, he immediately and reverently consumes all of the Blood of Christ that remains, assisted, if the case requires, by other **Deacons** and Priests. (*IGMR* 182)

The deacon is to minister the chalice (if it is to be offered). And, after communion, the remaining Precious Blood is consumed at the altar. If extraordinary ministers are also involved, it is my understanding that the deacon should still minister one of the chalices.

> The faithful should normally receive sacramental Communion of the Eucharist during Mass itself, at the moment laid down by the Rite of celebration, that is to say, just after the Priest celebrant's Communion. It is the Priest celebrant's responsibility to minister Communion, perhaps assisted by other Priests or **Deacons**; and he should not resume the Mass until after the Communion of the faithful is concluded. Only when there is a necessity may extraordinary ministers assist the Priest celebrant in accordance with the norm of law. (*RS*, 88)

A deacon should not delegate his responsibility to an extraordinary minister.

> ... It is to be noted that if the Priest or **Deacon** hands the sacred host or chalice to ... concelebrants, he says nothing; that is to say, he does not pronounce the words "The Body of Christ" or "The Blood of Christ." (*RS*, 98)

This instruction applies, of course, to only Masses with concelebrants, but deacons need to be aware of it.

After Communion

> … Where a **Deacon** is present, he returns with the Priest to the altar and purifies the vessels. It is permissible, however, especially if there are several vessels to be purified, to leave them, covered as may be appropriate, on a corporal on the altar or on the credence table, and for them to be purified by the Priest or **Deacon** immediately after Mass once the people have been dismissed. … (*RS*, 119)

The deacon shares responsibility in the purification and care of the vessels of Communion with the priest.

> Once the Prayer after Communion has been said, the **Deacon** makes brief announcements to the people, if indeed any need to be made, unless the Priest prefers to do this himself. (*IGMR* 184)

Announcements occur after the prayer (not before). If there are numerous items, the assembly could be invited to sit.

Communion to the Sick

> A Priest or **Deacon** … who takes the Most Holy Eucharist … in order to administer it as Communion for a sick person, should go insofar as possible directly from the place where the Sacrament is reserved to the sick person's home … Furthermore the Rite for the administration of Communion to the sick, as prescribed in the Roman Ritual, is always to be used. (*RS*, 133)

The importance of the ministry of Communion to the Sick is emphasized, implying its primacy over all other ministry or activity.

> As has already been recalled, "the only minister who can confect the Sacrament of the Eucharist *in persona Christi* is a validly ordained Priest." Hence the name "minister of the Eucharist" belongs properly to the Priest alone. Moreover,

also by reason of their sacred Ordination, the ordinary ministers of Holy Communion are the Bishop, the Priest and the **Deacon**, to whom it belongs therefore to administer Holy Communion to the lay members of Christ's faithful during the celebration of Mass. In this way their ministerial Office in the Church is fully and accurately brought to light, and the sign value of the Sacrament is made complete. (*RS*, 154)

Deacons are not lay people; they are sacred ministers. They exercise their sacred power in humility, but they do not artificially humble that which is sacred.

Responsibility and Integrity

Any Catholic, whether Priest or **Deacon** or lay member of Christ's faithful, has the right to lodge a complaint regarding a liturgical abuse to the diocesan Bishop or the competent Ordinary equivalent to him in law, or to the Apostolic See on account of the primacy of the Roman Pontiff. It is fitting, however, insofar as possible, that the report or complaint be submitted first to the diocesan Bishop. This is naturally to be done in truth and charity. (*RS*, 184)

Let all Christ's faithful participate in the Most Holy Eucharist as fully, consciously and actively as they can, honoring it lovingly by their devotion and the manner of their life. Let Bishops, Priests and **Deacons**, in the exercise of the sacred ministry, examine their consciences as regards the authenticity and fidelity of the actions they have performed in the name of Christ and the Church in the celebration of the Sacred Liturgy. Let each one of the sacred ministers ask himself, even with severity, whether he has respected the rights of the lay members of Christ's faithful, who confidently entrust themselves and their children to him, relying on him to fulfill for the faithful those sacred functions that the Church intends to carry out in celebrating the Sacred Liturgy at Christ's command. For each one should always remember that he is a servant of the Sacred Liturgy. (*RS*, 186)

There can be a tendency for deacons to shy away from involvement in necessary change. Do they serve the liturgy by neglecting significant departures from the formal instructions? Deacons are called to cover judgment with charity (that's the part of the significance of wearing the dalmatic over the stole), but they cannot neglect their duty.

Strategy and Tactics

Perhaps, given the duration of time since publication of the first translation of the *IGMR*, virtually all of the rubrics listed above have been satisfied in one's own parish – all the better.

However, should there be some dragging of feet towards cheerful compliance, what is the faithful deacon to do? Deacons make a vow of obedience to their ordinary at their ordination – where the bishop is, there is the Church. And, they are directed to fulfill their responsibility to faithfulness to the liturgy. Clearly, that which directly involves the deacon is to be his concern.

First, they must become thoroughly familiar with the *IGMR*, *RS*, and pertinent parts of the Missal, plus additional documents that relate to the liturgy in the United States – this article is not intended to be authoritative, but to point to that which is. In addition to the Vatican website (www.Vatican. va), the United States Conference of Catholic Bishops website (http://www.USCCB.org) has many of these resources. Also, additional documents of the individual diocese in which the deacon ministers may be relevant. Ideally, pastors, parochial vicars, and liturgy committees would be open to positive changes offered humbly and in accord with the new *IGMR* and *RS*. The latter makes clear which changes are most important. Some things deacons can easily do themselves: wear the cincture, faithfully proclaim the words of the Gospel, and correctly enunciate the appropriate texts.

Concerning the Book of the Gospels and dalmatic (one for each seasonal color, if the deacon or his parish does not have a complete set): There are several alternatives: (1) The deacons can prevail upon the pastor to purchase dalmatics and/or the Book of the Gospels (show him paragraphs 338 of the *IGMR* and 125 of *RS*). (2) If the deacon's personal financial situation permits, dalmatics in all four colors and, perhaps, even the Book of the Gospels could be purchased for personal use and/or for the parish. (3) If the married deacon's wife is an accomplished seamstress, perhaps she would be willing to sew dalmatics that match parish chasubles. (I know one deacon wife who produced four matching sets of dalmatics, chasubles, and stoles – long before the revised *IGMR* was published.) Whatever the solution, *we are strongly encouraged to wear the dalmatic at every Mass.*

If a flagon of wine is still consecrated during Mass, the deacon might suggest to the pastor, other priests, and/or liturgist that the wine be poured into chalices before Mass or during the preparation of the gifts instead – see *RS* paragraph 106. (My pastor, at the time and with the encouragement of the Archdiocesan Liturgy Office, introduced the latter change the weekend after *RS* was promulgated.)

If there are parts of the Mass that are proper to the deacon but exercised by another minister, or, conversely, parts that the deacon is exercising that are reserved to the priest, the deacon has a special challenge. For example, if the deacon has been introducing the *Mysterium Fidei* (Mystery of Faith), he needs to get with the other deacons (if there are more than one in the parish), gain consensus on the change, and then broach the subject with the pastor and other priests.

Then there's the more delicate situation – laypeople have been leading the Prayers of the Faithful for years. First of all, the deacon needs to get the support the pastor and other deacons, and then work with the person who trains the readers. In my own experience, as I trained the readers (who had been offering the Prayers), I was in a position to diplomatically and carefully (I trust) introduce the change (after the pastor had given me permission), especially referring to the revised *IGMR*. As I was the only deacon in the parish at the time, I was also in a position to remind the scheduled lector before each Mass I served. Change is not always easily achieved, but now that there are four deacons in my parish, readers are no longer expecting to lead the Prayers at most Masses (but are prepared, just in case).

And there's the other delicate problem – extraordinary ministers of Holy Communion may have been more involved at the altar than the revised instructions provide for. Again, the pastor and liturgy committee need to be involved. The extraordinary ministers (not "Eucharistic ministers"!) need to be carefully and sensitively catechized, especially in parishes in which the ministry of deacon has been recently introduced.

Deacons can lead their parishes into closer relationship with Christ and his Church – it is the primary motivation of our ministry. By facilitating faithful ministry of Word and Sacrament, through faithful implementation of the revised instructions, the ministry of Charity can be exercised even more effectively.

Making sense of the ministry of the deacon

(Slightly modified from the original published in Homiletic and Pastoral Review, 2006, http://www.catholicculture.org/culture/library/view.cfm?id=7428)

In the parish of my deacon assignment, I am given the opportunity to preach the homily on the order of one or two Masses per month. On occasion, I've had more than one parishioner thank me for the homily but then express a somewhat disconcerting opinion, which goes something like this: "You know, you deacons are so much more in touch with the 'real world'; priests should be married like you are, so they could understand what the 'world' is like and relate to us better." Rather than become engaged in prolonged debate, I quickly (but politely) disagree, with the practicalities first: most U.S. parishes are in no position to financially support a married priest and his family. More importantly, however, I do a quick catechesis, in the form of a rhetorical question: Would we rather have a priest who "knows and lives" the everyday struggles of married and family life or a priest who models the chaste spousal relationship of Christ and the Church? I conclude by saying that the ministries of priest and deacon are fundamentally different, even though the former incorporates the latter in more than a transitional way. I also may note that deacons need not be married. If I had more time in such an encounter, I would elaborate with the following kind of analysis of the ministry of the deacon:

Church Declarations

With the restoration of the permanent diaconate in the Latin Rite after Vatican Council II, the subsequent experience of the restored order – by deacons themselves, their pastors and bishops, and the parishes of their ministry – provides motivation for reflection on the significance of the ministry for the Church of the new century. Vatican II and post-conciliar documents have defined progressively elaborated on the nature and functions of the order, particularly in relation to the episcopacy and priesthood. In addition to the two other degrees of Orders, relation of the diaconate to the laity is worthy of reflection, also.

Until Vatican II, the primary focus of the sacrament of Holy Orders was the priesthood, especially as it related to Eucharist, and secondarily to Penance and Extreme Unction (Anointing of the Sick). The diaconate was understood as transitional to the priesthood, while even bishops emphasized their own priesthood. Beginning with the Council, and through subsequent documents, the Church progressively emphasizes the threefold hierarchy of Orders: episcopacy, priesthood, and diaconate:

> Bishops enjoy the fullness of the sacrament of orders and both presbyters and deacons are dependent upon them in the exercise of their authority. For the presbyters are the prudent fellow workers of the episcopal order and are themselves consecrated as true priests of the New Testament, just as deacons are ordained for the ministry and serve the people of God in communion with the bishop and his presbytery. (CD, 15)

> For strengthened by sacramental grace, in communion with the bishop and his group of priests [deacons,] serve in the diaconate of the liturgy, of the word, and of charity to the people of God. (LG, 29)

> ...the Second Ecumenical Vatican Council ... after concerning itself with the bishops and the priests ... praised also the third rank of sacred orders, explaining its dignity and enumerating its functions. (SDO)

The sacrament of apostolic ministry comprises three degrees. Indeed "the divinely instituted ecclesiastical ministry is exercised in different degrees by those who even from ancient times have been called bishops, priests and deacons". (BN, 1, citing *Ad pascendum*[AP])

Functionally and by identity, "[b]ishops enjoy the fullness of the sacrament of orders," (CD, 15) including the consummate power to ordain and the ordinary power to confirm, as well as the *munera* (assigned service, function, duty) of the priesthood and diaconate. Similarly, the priesthood includes preeminent power to preside over the Eucharist (confecting the sacred species), administer absolution, and anoint the sick, as well as provide pastoral care of the parish. The diaconate, the third rank of the hierarchy, includes the ordinary ministry of the sacrament of Baptism, proclamation of the Gospel, assistance at the altar, receipt of wedding vows, burial of the dead, distribution of the sacred species, viaticum to the dying, and minister of charity to the poor, along with teaching, preaching, and presiding over prayer and Scripture services. These ministries are summarized under the threefold commission of the deacon: "With regard to deacons, 'strengthened by sacramental grace they are dedicated to the People of God, in conjunction with the bishop and his body of priests, in the service (*diakonia*) of the **liturgy**, of the **Gospel** and of works of **charity**'". (*CCE*, 877)

In his first Encyclical, Benedict XVI writes, "As the years went by and the Church spread further afield, the exercise of **charity** became established as one of her essential activities, along with the administration of the **sacraments** and the proclamation of the **word**..." (*Deus Caritas Est,* **emphasis** added*.*) In the previous paragraph, he notes the ministry of the Seven (Acts 6), together with the example of Lawrence, deacon and martyr of Rome. The ministry of deacon – Word, altar, charity – is, then, the fundamental ministry (prophetic, priestly, and kingly) of the Church, with the priest and bishop possessing the deeper ministerial and pastoral responsibilities, especially Eucharist, *in persona Christi*. (*CCE*, 875)

Deacons are by virtue of ordination, clerics:

> Ministers of lesser rank are also sharers in the mission and grace of the Supreme Priest. In the first place among these ministers are deacons, who, in as much as they are dispensers of Christ's mysteries and servants of the Church, should keep themselves free from every vice and stand before men as personifications of goodness and friends of God. **Clerics**, who are called by the Lord and are set aside as

113

His portion in order to prepare themselves for the various ministerial offices under the watchful eye of spiritual shepherds, are bound to bring their hearts and minds into accord with this special election (which is theirs). They will accomplish this by their constancy in prayer, by their burning love, and by their unremitting recollection of whatever is true, just and of good repute. They will accomplish all this for the glory and honor of God. (*LG*, 41)

The Diaconate brings with it a series of rights and duties as defined by canons 273-283 of the 1983*CIC* with regard to clerics in general and deacons in particular. ... From the point of view of discipline, with diaconal ordination, the deacon is incardinated into a particular Church or personal prelature to whose service he has been admitted, or else, as a **cleric**, into a religious institute of consecrated life or a clerical society of apostolic life. (BN, 10)

The correspondence of the three-fold ministry of the deacon – Word, altar, charity – with the fundamental ministry of the Church is illuminative. For, the laity share in the ministry of the Church, as well:

[The laity] are by baptism made one body with Christ and are constituted among the People of God; they are in their own way made sharers in the priestly, prophetical, and kingly functions of Christ; and they carry out for their own part the mission of the whole Christian people in the Church and in the world. (*LG*, 31)

A common confusion seen in all corners of the Church concerns the status and identity of the deacon in relation to the priesthood and the laity. It is not uncommon to see the misnomer "lay deacon" applied, in not only secular publications, but even occasional even diocesan newspapers. Deacons themselves may describe their role as having "one foot in the clerical world and the other in the lay," clearly conflicting with the documents cited above. In many dioceses in the United States, deacons, who are nevertheless clerics, are discouraged by their bishops (certainly within their rights by Canon Law) and/or pastors from wearing clerical attire while formally ministering; conversely, where permitted or even encouraged, many deacons still resist donning a clerical shirt for ministry.

If we consider some other attributes of the deacon, in light of the three-fold ministry of deacon and Church, perhaps this might motivate better understanding of the diaconate.

> Insofar as it is a grade of holy orders, the diaconate imprints a **character** and communicates a specific **sacramental grace**. The diaconal character is the configurative and distinguishing sign indelibly impressed in the soul, which configures the one ordained to **Christ**, who made himself the deacon or **servant of all**. It brings with it a specific sacramental grace, which is strength, *vigor specialis*, a gift for living the new reality wrought by the sacrament. (BN, 12, quoting *CCE*, 876, 877)

> The **spirituality of service is a spirituality of the whole Church**, insofar as the whole Church, in the same way as Mary, is the "handmaid of the Lord" (Lk 1:28), at the service of the salvation of the world. And so that the whole Church may better live out this spirituality of service, the Lord gives her **a living and personal sign** of his very being as servant... In fact, with sacred ordination, he [the deacon] is constituted **a living icon of Christ the servant** within the Church. (BN, 1)

Experience

In parts of the United States where the permanent diaconate has not been restored, anecdotal accounts indicate that there are two primary motivations discouraging restoration: fear of negative effects on priestly vocations and lay ministry. A typical question, heard in such dioceses (and many parishes in dioceses with the diaconate, too) might be, "Why do we need deacons? Laypeople can do whatever needs to be done."

The answer to the preceding question might be expressed in particular, practical dimensions of diaconal ministry. In the Roman Rite, deacons, together with bishops and priests, are ordinary ministers of Baptism. And, it is through the initial sacrament that the call of Christ the Servant comes: the baptized are called to serve God and neighbor. It is through *diakonia* that the minister of Baptism – bishop, priest, deacon, or even, in emergency, a layperson – communicates the call. At the beginning of Mass, the deacon may lead the assembly in penance-pleading the mercy of Christ on his people-concluded with the (non-sacramental) forgiveness of sins offered by the priest. At the altar, the deacon visibly serves, and, as he kneels from the Epiclesis through the first elevation of the chalice, (*IGMR*, 179) leads the rest of the assembly in adoration as Christ becomes especially Real under the appearance of the gifts of bread and wine. (The deacon's ordination also involved an epiclesis, the invocation of the Holy Spirit over the kneeling ordinand that strengthens the gifts received at Confirmation.) The deacon elevates and ministers the chalice, the Blood of the new Covenant, shed for the forgiveness of sins. He invites the Sign of Peace.

We deacons serve God and his people. As we serve, we image Christ, who "did not come to be served but to serve" (Mt 20:28), and we serve Christ: "whatever you did for one of these least brothers of mine, you did for me" (Mt 25:40). We communicate by Word and sacrament the call to serve, to all the baptized. And, what of the bishops who send us and the priests whom we assist? The commission of service is intrinsic to the ordination rites to the priesthood and episcopate. The dalmatic (the outer vestment peculiar to the deacon) is sometimes worn under the chasuble by the bishop. The Mandatum of Holy Thursday, symbolizing that he who leads must first serve, is performed by priest and bishop, divested of chasuble and stole. The primary ministry of the deacon is still very much present in the other two orders, but "hidden" within the mystery of Christ the High Priest. The deacon makes the image of Christ the Servant visible.

Where was *diakonia* during the centuries in which the permanent deacon was largely absent? As noted above, in each age the Spirit raised up charismatic leaders from out of the monasteries and from the secular priesthood and laity to provide the service ministry that is *diakonia,* largely through existing and new religious orders. Francis of Assisi, one of the few permanent deacons of the Middle Ages, is the exception that proves the rule. In our own time, *diakonia* is no longer restricted to the charitable religious orders, but is beginning in our own time to flower in the parishes (but how many seeds still need sowing?) It is the deacon who makes the call visible and, together with his bishop and priests, plants, waters, and nourishes. The service to which all are called through Baptism is manifest in the exercise of charisms, while, for the ordained, in effect the charisms are to be "ordinary": they are *munera*. The Spirit is moving the parish in a new direction, and bishops are sending deacons to make visible the way.

The *munera* bestowed on the deacon: proclaiming, preaching, and teaching the Gospel, administering baptism, receiving wedding vows, burying the dead, custodian of the Most Blessed Sacrament, viaticum to the dying, care of the sick, and concern for the poor are still very much the responsibility of the priest and bishop. (The latter, of course, confers the *munera.*) Might it be said that when priest of bishop exercise any of these ministries, its exercise flows out of his own diaconal ordination, while overlain *in persona Christi capitis*?

Benedict XVI reminds us that *diakonia* is part of the essential commission of the Church. With the restoration of the permanent diaconate and its faithful exercise, *diakonia* is, once again, made sacramentally visible in the Western Church. The priest is celebrant of the central mysteries of the Faith; the deacon (married or celibate) serves the mysteries and, together with the laity, bears them into the "real world."

Eyes and ears

In regards to bishops and deacons, the "Apostolic Constitutions," a Third Century compilation of Church teachings, laws, and traditions (probably Syrian) reads:

> *That the **deacon** is to ease the burden of the bishops, and to order the smaller matters himself.*

> XLIV. Be of one mind, O bishops, one with one another, and be at peace with one another; sympathize with one another, love the brethren, and feed the people with care; with one consent teach those that are under you to be of the same sentiments and to be of the same opinions about the same matters, 'that there may be no schisms among you; that you may be one body and one spirit, perfectly joined together in the same mind and in the same judgment," according to the appointment of the Lord. And let the **deacon** refer all things to the bishop, as Christ does to His Father. But let him order such things as he is able by himself, receiving power from the bishop, as the Lord did from His Father the power of creation and of providence. But the weighty matters let the bishop judge; but let the **deacon** be the bishop's ear, and eye, and mouth, and heart and soul, that the bishop may not be distracted with many cares, but with such only as are more considerable, as Jethro did appoint for Moses, and his counsel was received. (Apostolic Constitutions IV, Roberts and Donaldson, 1899, slightly updated to contemporary English by the author)

"But let the deacon be the bishop's ear, and eye." is often cited in relation to the ministry of deacons and their special relationship with the bishop, who sends them forth. Yet, in a diocese with one hundred or even hundreds of deacons and many, many parishes, it is difficult to see how such a proclamation is practical; it even seems anachronistic, in that the relationship of deacon to bishop in the early Church seems to have been much closer than what is typical of today. Except perhaps bishops with less than say forty deacons, it

119

is not possible for a him to know each of deacon individually. For example, in the Church of Rome we have the traditional witness of Pope St. Sixtus and four of his deacons who were martyred together by Emperoro Valerian, shortly followed by two more deacons on the same day, and then a few days later, St. Lawrence, the last of the seven deacons, who suffered the legendary gridiron.

In my diocese there just under 200 deacons. Several dioceses have many more. It is clearly difficult for the ordinary of the archdiocese to get to know all of these men and to have regular, ongoing one–on–one interaction. Like other dioceses with large numbers of deacons, the bishop would be challenged to to know and remember each man's name. (The beloved bishop who ordained me, may he rest in peace, repeatedly called me "Max" during formation; happily he remembered my name at and after ordination.) Most deacons are assigned to parishes, so perhaps the statement, "eyes and ears of the bishop" might be augmented by "eyes and ears of the pastor," as well, without diminishing the relationship of deacon and bishop.

In my own ministry, I often find myself "drumming up business" for the priest – especially the sacraments of reconciliation and anointing of the sick. A conversation might go something like this:

> After daily Mass, a man asks me, "Deacon, please pray for my wife. She's going in for knee replacement surgery next week."
>
> I respond, "I sure will. Has her knee been bothering her for a while? – I've seen her with a cane for several months."
>
> "Yes," he says, "and now she can barely make it to Sunday Mass, much less daily Mass, so I've been coming alone for some time."
>
> Me: "You know, if she can't make it to Mass this Sunday, or while she's recovering, please call the office, and either I or an extraordinary minister of Holy Communion can bring Communion to her."

Him: "I'll do that deacon. Well, have a good…"

I interrupt him: "Before you go, has your wife been anointed – you know the Sacrament of the Sick? Before that big surgery I had a few years ago, I received the anointing. It's recommended before any surgery like this or when anyone has a significant illness."

Him: "You know, I don't think she has been anointed ever."

Me: "Well, you ask her – tell her that the deacon wants her to be anointed."

Him, smiling: "I will – and I'll call Father once she gives the okay."

Me: "And let me know how the surgery goes. I'll be praying. The Lord is good. And tell her hello for me."

Him: "Will do."

I'm not going to give an example of what a conversation might lead to my suggesting the Sacrament of Reconciliation. Obviously, helping another to recognize potential sinfulness is a very delicate, unique matter. I'm in no position to judge, but what I can do is relate what the Church teaches about matters such as abortion, contraception, or unforgiveness, and, at the same time, emphasize the great mercy we have in Christ Jesus, the forgiveness he offers to those who sincerely repent, and the healing we receive in Confession. To the person who is reluctant to personally confess to a priest, I may recount one of my own experiences:

A few years before I entered deacon formation, I and my wife had encounters with the Lord which led us to deeper commitments of service to him and his Church. Shortly thereafter, our older daughter was in second grade; it was Advent, and the evening of her First Reconciliation, for which our parish offered a communal penance service, with many priests from nearby parishes in addition to our own. With no little pride, we took her and her two younger brothers to the service. Each family was encouraged to bring their child forth followed by their parents and older siblings. Our younger son, only about two, was asleep on my shoulder, while our other son held my wife's hand. (Our two youngest had not yet come on the scene.) It was memorable, certainly, because of the step forward our oldest child was making in her walk with the Lord, although, no, I don't remember what sins I confessed that night.

The next week, we were clearing off the dinner table. We had a familiar Advent/Christmas decoration, Swedish angel chimes – four small candles generating heat which, rising, drive a rotating metal fan, on the outside of which are four cherubs, heralding the coming of the King, with little clappers hanging down and ringing three little bells. As I listened to the bells, it was as if I heard them sing, "Come and go with me to my master's house," over and over again. I said to my wife, "This may sound crazy, but I think we are to go back to Church tonight, for the parish-wide penance service." The previous week's service had been oriented towards First Reconciliation children and their families.

So, there we went, the five of us, back to Church. Our poor daughter was already celebrating her "Second Reconciliation." No, again I cannot remember what sins I confessed, but I do remember the experience I had as I returned to my seat after receiving absolution. I suddenly felt myself overcome by a profound affection for, love of everyone present in that Church. I felt *reconciled.* For the first time I had an intuitive, experiential understanding of the Sacrament which had escaped me before. Confession is meant to, and when sincerely received, actually accomplish reconciliation of the penitent not only with God, but with his people. The priest represents not only Christ Jesus, who forgives the sinner, but also his Body, the Church, which also forgives the prodigal, welcoming him or her back into the flock.

Of course, if the deacon is going to be actively boarding penititents and sick people for the priest-captain (from *capitis*), the latter has to be at the helm of the ship of forgiveness and healing.

The real challenge in a parish is not so much being aware of the sick and elderly, but picking up on issues of pain and misunderstanding.

Separation, divorce, and re marriage outside of the Church are all too common. When preparing young people for marriage, I try to wrap up their preparation with an anticipatory blessing of sorts. I tell them that should they, in future years of their marriage, become discouraged or hurt or have "fallen out of love," that their first stop on the way "out of their marriage" is not the office of an attorney, but, rather, my office or that of another deacon or priest. I so much want and pray them to remember what they heard from me and from the others who prepared them. The Church is not only the place where we celebrate the great sacramental milestones of our faith – baptism, communion, confirmation, marriage, it's also the place where the pain of the heart can be healed, where forgiveness overflows, and the great mercy of God is experienced. Between the homily, sacramental preparation, adult catechetics, and one-on-one conversation, the deacon is there to be the herald of invitation to the great celebration, the wedding feast of the Lamb.

Deacon formation

So what might a man expect if he is accepted into diaconate formation? Quite simply, every diocese that has a diaconate formation program is different. Even if a diocese, in the United States for example, is making every effort to conform to the norms of the National Directory, the means by which such conformity is achieved certainly may vary from diocese to diocese.

The norms defined by the US National Directory involve criteria to be met for each stage of a man's deacon formation. Initially, there are specific expectations based on Canon Law, as discussed above. If there are no canonical impediments, then there is recommendation by his pastor for the man to enter formation. Ideally, the pastor should be aware of the canonical criteria and utilize them in deciding whether to recommend the application of one of his parishioners for the diaconate. Standard documentation, in addition to pastors' recommendations, includes: (1) Recently obtained Baptismal certificate from parish of Baptism, with notations of Confirmation, and, possibly, marriage, or equivalent documentation for converts, (2) marriage license (if married), (3) evidence of citizenship (birth certificate or passport) or residency (green card in the United States), (4) education diplomas and transcripts (the minimum national requirement is a high school diploma; some dioceses may require bachelor degrees), (5) the actual applications, which may also include autobiographies (if married, wives' also), and (6) statements indicating approval of spouses to enter formation (typically, at each step of formation, the wives' approvals are required for continuation, again, if married).

Upon admission, formation proceeds in well–defined steps, beginning with the "aspirancy period," typically one year, in which the primary focus is on discernment – is the aspirant truly called to the diaconate? The principal dimensions of formation: intellectual, human, spiritual, and pastoral are introduced in scheduled classes and in-parish assignments. Some dioceses schedule in-class work on weekday evenings while others schedule weekend formation; usually the geographic extent of the diocese is the controlling factor. The National Directory for the United States calls for adult-style of learning and formation in which each man takes responsibility for his own formation, while formators (typically deacons and priests) engage each man as facilitators as well as evaluators in the integrated formation and discernment process.

Typical formation consists of college-level courses in each of the key areas of intellectual formation: Sacred Scripture, philosophy, moral, dogmatic, and sacramental (initiation, matrimony, and orders) theology, Christology, liturgy, Canon Law (with emphasis on orders, initiation, and matrimony). Ideally, human, spiritual, and pastoral dimensions are integrated in varying degrees with intellectual formation.

No matter the diocese, there is much to study, with the Catechism of the Catholic Church typically providing the foundation. Men study the Sacraments (especially Baptism, Confirmation, Eucharist, Matrimony and Holy Orders), Sacred Scripture, Church history, Dogmatic and Moral Theology, the writings of the (early) Church Fathers, Documents of Vatican Council II, and the *CIC*, especially those canons relevant to the Sacraments of Initiation, Matrimony, and Orders. As would be expected, the diaconate, itself, is the primary target of study. Practica (e.g., instruction and practice) of liturgical service, ministry of charity, and parochial formation, within or outside of the home parish, help to integrate formation. (Many resources are available online, including the *CCE*, *CIC*, Bible, Documents of Vatican II, and writings of the Fathers and medieval scholars (e.g., Aquinas and Bonaventure). (Should prospective deacons be assigned essays, the simplicity of copying and pasting from electronic documents is a great blessing. However, it can be a temptation to plagiarize as well; always cite the source and focus on understanding.)

Dioceses around the United States are in varying stages of adapting their formation programs to comply with the norms of the National Directory. In some cases dioceses which lacked an active diaconate are in the process of implementing formation for the first time.

What might a man expect of the deacon formation program in his diocese? Perhaps it is worthwhile to recall the response of Jesus to Andrew and the other disciple's query, "Rabbi, where are you staying." He said, "Come and you will see." (John 1:38-39).

Young or old?

When might a man hear the call to the diaconate? In my archdiocese we see men in their early thirties and through mid-sixties invited into diaconate formation. In the United States, the minimum age for ordination to the permanent diaconate is thirty-five, whether the man is married or celibate. This means that, for a four-plus-year formation program, men younger than thirty-one are not yet admitted. Many dioceses have introduced a maximum age for entrance into formation and/or ordination.

From a personal perspective, I observe men who are active in fruitful ministry into their late seventies or even eighties, although it is acknowledged that they would have difficulty with a formation program at that age; in a sense they are "cruising" on the accumulated grace of years of diaconal service which allows for inspiring preaching and wise counsel. By the same token, I have observed men who upon ordination are in their sixties, and, even though the duration of their ministry may be short, they still provide the grace of diaconal witness that is beyond measure of the "cost" of their formation. And, of course, there is the mystery of the indelible character imprinted on the deacon – a sign which he is to bear into eternal life; might a short diaconal service in this life be an anticipation of a glorified service in the next? Nevertheless, it is recognized that the norms of the National Directory are oriented towards ministry in the current life, and, therefore, prudence implies that potential candidates be in good physical health as well as living a faithful Catholic life of service to God and neighbor.

The potential of a man being thirty-five upon ordination, together with a faithful life of service, is not enough for his own self-evaluation of his call. He may indeed be called to ordained ministry, but, perhaps not yet. If a man has a young, growing family, he, together with his wife, must prayerfully discern his possible entry into formation. How would formation and, later, ordination affect his family? Would formation and/or the ministry stress his family life too much, especially with young children? Or conversely, might formation and the ministry enrich his family life? While dad is gone to formation class, occasionally accompanied by mom, how would the children get along? Each married couple would have to answer these questions together. I can only state my own experience: the adventure of formation and ministry was something that our entire family shared, even with our youngest barely one year old upon my ordination. My wife and I were so convinced of my call that we found creative ways to adapt family life to the diaconate.

Some applicants with young families might find those evaluating their application with a jaundiced eye, precisely because of the demands young children make on mother and father. A jaundiced eye is not, however, a measure of discernment. Applicants and their wives, of any age or family circumstance, need to have that conviction of that call and how they would adapt their life to formation and ministry, in order to convince the skeptics they might encounter. Even further, they must convince themselves, whether or not they encounter doubt in others.

To summarize, men with young families and more mature men on the verge of retirement need not be excluded from the ministry of deacon, if they and their wives (if married), are convinced of the call and can adequately demonstrate the strength of their convictions to the admitting committee.

Scriptural and liturgical reflections

The exercises below are written as if a deacon after many years of service were looking back at how God has used him in so many ways.

For the man who is not yet ordained, they can be viewed in several ways. (1) For the "possible" deacon, that man who is trying to decide whether to apply, (2) for the Aspirant as he studies his way through a year of study, (3) for the Candidate as Ordination approaches through the ministries of Lector and Acolyte. Further, the imagination of the could-be deacon is to be engaged in two ways — putting himself in the place of the experienced deacon and reflecting on his ministry over the years.

Elevation

Immediately after the words of institution and the elevation of first the Sacred Body and then the chalice of the Precious Blood, which the deacon has witnessed while kneeling, the deacon stands. And, he, with the assembly, joins with the celebrant as all chant (one of the three options, such as):

> When we eat this Bread and drink the Cup, we proclaim your Death, O Lord, until you come again.

The celebrant continues the Eucharistic Prayer until he reaches the end and takes up the ciborium while the deacon raises the chalice, as the celebrant alone chants,

> Through him, and with him, and in him, O God, almighty Father, in the unity of the Holy Spirit, all glory and honor is yours for ever and ever.

> All respond,

> Amen (amen, amen...).

As the deacon holds aloft that chalice, can he not help but remember the Psalm (116:12-13):

> How can I repay the LORD for all the good done for me?

I will raise the cup of salvation and call on the name of the LORD.

Is this not for which I was ordained, he asks? The Lord has indeed been good to me. He has given me life, wife, family... He has given me Himself, first in the washing-away of inherited sin by my baptism which welcomed me into his Church, in the faith he has gifted me to exercise through the sacraments, above all in the Eucharist which nourishes my soul. He has given me this marvelous ministry. How can I make a return to him for all this goodness? By calling on him to gift me ever more completely, that I may serve Him and His people in even greater love and mercy.

Can the man who contemplates the ministry of deacon imagine himself in that role – one who bears the weight of the chalice filled with the Precious Blood of his Lord?

Gifts

As the deacon remembers the bishop praying for an even greater outpouring of the gift of the Spirit at the candidate's ordination, the deacon considers how those gifts have been experienced as he preached and proclaimed the Gospel, and ministered to the poor and hurting, and fed the people with His Precious Blood. The eyes of faith can see the gifts poured out on and through the Messiah flowing through the words and actions of the deacon.

> But a shoot shall sprout from the stump of Jesse, and from his roots a bud shall blossom.

> The spirit of the LORD shall rest upon him: a spirit of wisdom and of understanding, A spirit of counsel and of strength, a spirit of knowledge and of fear of the LORD, and his delight shall be the fear of the LORD. (Isaiah 11:1-4)

Servant

What does it mean to be a servant, a minister of the altar, of the Word, of charity? Are there amazing things which come about as the deacon becomes the icon of Christ the servant?

Here is my servant whom I uphold, my chosen one with whom I am pleased, Upon whom I have put my spirit; he shall bring forth justice to the nations, Not crying out, not shouting, not making his voice heard in the street. A bruised reed he shall not break, and a smoldering wick he shall not quench, Until he establishes justice on the earth; the coastlands will wait for his teaching. (Isaiah 42:1-4)

Efficacy

Where is the sacramentality of the deacon? How does the deacon manifest that efficacy that is intrinsic to each of the other sacraments? When the water (the matter) is poured and the words (the form) of the Rite of Baptism are said, that which is symbolized is actually accomplished (the Spirit hovering as a new Creation comes into existence, the washing away of Original Sin, being freed of slavery to sin, crossing over the Jordan into the Promised Land of the Church). When the laying on of hands of the bishop (the matter) and the words of the Epiclesis (the form) are said over the diaconal candidate, he truly acquires an indelible character that transforms him into a deacon, strengthened by the gifts of the Spirit for the ministry. As the deacon ministers, he "feels" in faith that strength – that new identity, the icon of Christ the Servant. The words actually accomplish that which the laying on of hands symbolizes.

All you who are thirsty, come to the water! You who have no money, come, receive grain and eat; Come, without paying and without cost, drink wine and milk! ...

For my thoughts are not your thoughts, nor are your ways my ways, says the LORD.

As high as the heavens are above the earth, so high are my ways above your ways and my thoughts above your thoughts.

For just as from the heavens the rain and snow come down And do not return there till they have watered the earth, making it fertile and fruitful, Giving seed to him who sows and bread to him who eats,

So shall my word be that goes forth from my mouth;

It shall not return to me void, but shall do my will, achieving the end for which I sent it. (Isaiah 55:1,9-11)

In what ways can the deacon recognize that through his ministry the Gospel of the Lord was proclaimed and efficaciously transformed those who received that ministry?

Inflation

Can the deacon perform the tasks of his ministry without becoming either inflated or deflated? How can he exercise his faith that his words and actions are indeed effective, not because of his own worth and value, but by the Spirit working through him? Consider Mark's response:

> They came to Capernaum and, once inside the house, he began to ask them, "What were you arguing about on the way?" But they remained silent. They had been discussing among themselves on the way who was the greatest. Then he sat down, called the Twelve, and said to them, "If anyone wishes to be first, he shall be the last of all and the servant of all." (Mark 9:33-35)

Or Luke's account:

> Then an argument broke out among them about which of them should be regarded as the greatest. He said to them, "The kings of the Gentiles lord it over them and those in authority over them are addressed as 'Benefactors'; but among you it shall not be so. Rather, let the greatest among you be as the youngest, and the leader as the servant.
>
> For who is greater: the one seated at table or the one who serves? Is it not the one seated at table? I am among you as the one who serves. (Luke 22:24-27)

Prepare

The deacon wonders how he can be that alert, faithful servant, not merely for his own good, but for all of his family and parish.

> "Gird your loins and light your lamps and be like servants who await their master's return from a wedding, ready to open immediately when he comes and knocks. Blessed are those servants whom the master finds vigilant on his arrival. Amen, I say to you, he will gird himself, have them recline at table, and proceed to wait on them. And should he come in the second or third watch and find them prepared in this way, blessed are those servants. Be sure of this: if the master of the house had known the hour when the thief was coming, he would not have let his house be broken into. You also must be prepared, for at an hour you do not expect, the Son of Man will come."

> Then Peter said, "Lord, is this parable meant for us or for everyone?"

> And the Lord replied, "Who, then, is the faithful and prudent steward whom the master will put in charge of his servants to distribute (the) food allowance at the proper time? Blessed is that servant whom his master on arrival finds doing so. Truly, I say to you, he will put him in charge of all his property. But if that servant says to himself, 'My master is delayed in coming,' and begins to beat the menservants and the maidservants, to eat and drink and get drunk, then that servant's master will come on an unexpected day and at an unknown hour and will punish him severely and assign him a place with the unfaithful. That servant who knew his master's will but did not make preparations nor act in accord with his will shall be beaten severely; and the servant who was ignorant of his master's will but acted in a way deserving of a severe beating shall be beaten only lightly. Much will be required of the person entrusted with much, and still more will be demanded of the person entrusted with more. (Luke 12:35-48)

Talent

Can the deacon be trusted to invest the gifts of his ordination, bestowed on top of his baptism and his confirmation, to build up that part of the kingdom with which he has been entrusted?

While they were listening to him speak, he proceeded to tell a parable because he was near Jerusalem and they thought that the kingdom of God would appear there immediately.

So he said, "A nobleman went off to a distant country to obtain the kingship for himself and then to return. He called ten of his servants and gave them ten gold coins and told them, 'Engage in trade with these until I return.' His fellow citizens, however, despised him and sent a delegation after him to announce, 'We do not want this man to be our king.' But when he returned after obtaining the kingship, he had the servants called, to whom he had given the money, to learn what they had gained by trading. The first came forward and said, 'Sir, your gold coin has earned ten additional ones.' He replied, 'Well done, good servant! You have been faithful in this very small matter; take charge of ten cities.' Then the second came and reported, 'Your gold coin, sir, has earned five more.' And to this servant too he said, 'You, take charge of five cities.' Then the other servant came and said, 'Sir, here is your gold coin; I kept it stored away in a handkerchief, for I was afraid of you, because you are a demanding person; you take up what you did not lay down and you harvest what you did not plant.' He said to him, 'With your own words I shall condemn you, you wicked servant. You knew I was a demanding person, taking up what I did not lay down and harvesting what I did not plant; why did you not put my money in a bank? Then on my return I would have collected it with interest.' And to those standing by he said, 'Take the gold coin from him and give it to the servant who has ten.' But they said to him, 'Sir, he has ten gold coins.' 'I tell you, to everyone who has, more will be given, but from the one who has not, even what he has will be taken away. '" (Luke 19:11-26)

Mandate

Revisiting an observation above, isn't it remarkable that it is the pastor who, on Holy Thursday, reenacts the *Mandatum*, which one might think properly belongs to the deacon? Of course, the priest removes the chasuble before the action, as if he is unveiling his diaconal ordination (and the parish deacons assist him):

> Before the feast of Passover, Jesus knew that his hour had come to pass from this world to the Father. He loved his own in the world and he loved them to the end. The devil had already induced Judas, son of Simon the Iscariot, to hand him over. So, during supper, fully aware that the Father had put everything into his power and that he had come from God and was returning to God, he rose from supper and took off his outer garments. He took a towel and tied it around his waist. Then he poured water into a basin and began to wash the disciples' feet and dry them with the towel around his waist. He came to Simon Peter, who said to him, "Master, are you going to wash my feet?" Jesus answered and said to him, "What I am doing, you do not understand now, but you will understand later." Peter said to him, "You will never wash my feet." Jesus answered him, "Unless I wash you, you will have no inheritance with me." Simon Peter said to him, "Master, then not only my feet, but my hands and head as well." Jesus said to him, "Whoever has bathed has no need except to have his feet washed, for he is clean all over; so you are clean, but not all." For he knew who would betray him; for this reason, he said, "Not all of you are clean."
>
> So when he had washed their feet (and) put his garments back on and reclined at table again, he said to them, "Do you realize what I have done for you? You call me 'teacher' and 'master,' and rightly so, for indeed I am. If I, therefore,

137

the master and teacher, have washed your feet, you ought to wash one another's feet. I have given you a model to follow, so that as I have done for you, you should also do. Amen, amen, I say to you, no slave is greater than his master nor any messenger greater than the one who sent him. If you understand this, blessed are you if you do it". (John 13:1-17)

In what ways does the deacon daily "wash the feet" of those whom he encounters through his life and ministry?

Need

What is the need for deacons in this, the Twenty-first Century of Our Lord? The proto-deacons of the sixth chapter of the Acts of the Apostles were needed to minister to the minority Greek-speaking widows among the early Jewish Christians; soon they were called by the Spirit to bring the good news to Samaritans and foreigners, as well as give their lives over for the Savior. The fathers at Vatican Council II recognized a need, do you?

> At that time, as the number of disciples continued to grow, the Hellenists complained against the Hebrews because their widows were being neglected in the daily distribution.

> So the Twelve called together the community of the disciples and said, "It is not right for us to neglect the word of God to serve at table. Brothers, select from among you seven reputable men, filled with the Spirit and wisdom, whom we shall appoint to this task, whereas we shall devote ourselves to prayer and to the ministry of the word."

> The proposal was acceptable to the whole community, so they chose Stephen, a man filled with faith and the holy Spirit, also Philip, Prochorus, Nicanor, Timon, Parmenas, and Nicholas of Antioch, a convert to Judaism. They presented these men to the apostles who prayed and laid hands on them.

138

The word of God continued to spread, and the number of the disciples in Jerusalem increased greatly; even a large group of priests were becoming obedient to the faith. (Acts 6:1-7)

The experienced deacon asks himself how he has become an instrument of service as did the proto-deacons.

Response
The married deacon has the additional responsibility of wife and family which came before. He is to minister as deacon and husband and father to them first, ahead of the rest of the Church. How can he do this?

> Be subordinate to one another out of reverence for Christ. Wives should be subordinate to their husbands as to the Lord. For the husband is head of his wife just as Christ is head of the church, he himself the savior of the body. As the church is subordinate to Christ, so wives should be subordinate to their husbands in everything.
>
> Husbands, love your wives, even as Christ loved the church and handed himself over for her to sanctify her, cleansing her by the bath of water with the word, that he might present to himself the church in splendor, without spot or wrinkle or any such thing, that she might be holy and without blemish. So (also) husbands should love their wives as their own bodies. He who loves his wife loves himself. For no one hates his own flesh but rather nourishes and cherishes it, even as Christ does the church, because we are members of his body. "For this reason a man shall leave (his) father and (his) mother and be joined to his wife, and the two shall become one flesh."
>
> This is a great mystery, but I speak in reference to Christ and the church.

In any case, each one of you should love his wife as himself, and the wife should respect her husband. (Ephesians 5:22-33)

As the wife subordinates herself to her husband, he, in imitation of the Bridegroom of the Church, is to lay down his life for his bride. (The celibate priest sees his parish as his bride for whom he is to sacrifice himself.)

Empty

Ultimately, is not the deacon to be willing to offer everything for and to the Lord, in imitation of him?

> Have among yourselves the same attitude that is also yours in Christ Jesus,
>
> Who, though he was in the form of God, did not regard equality with God something to be grasped.
>
> Rather, he emptied himself, taking the form of a slave, coming in human likeness; and found human in appearance, he humbled himself, becoming obedient to death, even death on a cross. (Philippians 2:1-7)

Tentative conclusion: Who is called?

An individual man, by his nature, may be called. Indeed, many, many more might be called to ordained ministry. *You*, the non-ordained male reader may be hearing that call.

However, you first need to acknowledge you indeed *may* be called. In the internal rhyme of the previous statement, "need" indeed requires verification; you need to discern that possibility, with your wife (if you are married), with your pastor, and with those assigned responsibility for the formation of deacons, including, quite possibly early on, but certainly and finally, your bishop. I believe that many more men, mostly married, are being called to the diaconate or (among the celibate) even the priesthood, than are responding to the call.

Assuming a man satisfies all of the canonical requirements: appropriate age, faithfully living an orthodox Catholic life, married no more than one time, if married the wife agrees, faithful husband and father (if married and with a family), capable of college-level study, employment is not counter to Catholic teaching, mentally stable, literate, computer competent (if not savvy) ... why not the diaconate?

If the answer is, "I don't feel called," that answer requires further queries with honest, deep reflective responses."

Why do you believe that you are *not* called?"	
Potential answers might include:	**Response**
My diocese doesn't have deacons.	What if your bishop, tomorrow, announced that a formation program for deacons will begin in the next year?
	Would you be prepared to explore the possibility of the diaconate in the future?
	Might you be in a position to suggest

	that your bishop consider adding diaconal ministry to the service of his diocese?
My current job wouldn't permit time for either formation or deacon ministry.	What if your job changed? If you had a deeper sense of call, could you change your job?
(If married) My wife doesn't want me to consider this ministry.	This is a definitive answer, unless your wife can and does change her mind. For the purpose of strengthening your marriage, aside from the diaconate vocation, you might want to reflect on the "why" of her opposition: is it possible that you could be devoting much more husband/father time and presence with your wife and family than you currently are? Are you listening to her with your heart? Do not allow her opposition to affect your marriage. If she says "no" and that's final, you can (and should) let go of your desire for ordination – you're truly *not* called.
I'm satisfied with my current ministry responsibilities in my parish.	Is God satisfied with your ministry? Might He be asking more of you?
I understand that a deacon has to make a promise of obedience to the bishop before ordination. I don't think I want to be responsible to	What about your pastor; doesn't your ministry depend on him? Are you currently obedient to the commandments of the Lord? Do you make every effort to conform your life to the teachings of the

anyone else when it comes to my ministry.	Church? What does this "obedience," to which you don't want to conform yourself, really mean? Are you listening to the Lord through the Church?
I do not believe I am worthy enough to be ordained?	What are the gifts and talents which the Lord has endowed you with that you can be, and perhaps are, sharing with your brothers and sisters of the faith? How would you feel about having these gifts and talents strengthened by the Holy Spirit so you could more effectively exercise them? Do you understand the nature of ordained ministry – its purpose is not to elevate or inflate the deacon or the priest, but to empower him to minister humbly to God's people? What does it mean to have as Lord one who came not to be served but to serve?
I don't *feel* the call.	Do you make decisions in your life entirely about how you *feel*? Or do you try to reason things out before deciding what to do? Do you understand that the Catholic Christian belief is a combination of faith and reason, believing that God's grace builds on nature? What is that experience you would

	look for that would make you *feel* as if you are receiving a call? Discernment is the gift that both Church and inquirer should pray for. Look at your feeling – what is responsible for it?

The series of hypothetical dialogues above (between you and God; if married – also involving your wife) are not exhaustive, of course, but what they illustrate are some of the elements of discernment that go into deciding, in this case, whether one may be called to the diaconate. And, even if one goes through a deep discernment process, that man will also have to entrust the decision of advancement and ultimately ordination to others, including (if married) his wife and some of whom might not necessarily agree with the man's discernment.

One of the other remarkable developments in the post-Vatican II Church is the progressive involvement of more and more lay people in Church ministry. Where, formerly, vowed religious dominated religious education, in both parish and Order-run schools and parish religious education programs, more and more lay people are involved, in some cases by necessity, with the dramatic decrease in the number of religious. And, there are significantly greater numbers of lay people involved in Catholic higher education, including seminaries. This brings forth an interesting point, already explored above. The Fathers of Vatican Council II write:

> ... Now, in order to plant the Church and to make the Christian community grow, various ministries are needed, which are raised up by divine calling from the midst of the faithful congregation, and are to be carefully fostered and tended to by all. Among these are the offices of priests, of deacons, and of catechists, and Catholic action.

> ... [To repeat...]there are men who actually carry out the functions of the deacon's office ... It is only right to strengthen them by the imposition of hands which has come

down from the Apostles, and to bind them more closely to the altar, that they may carry out their ministry more effectively because of the sacramental grace of the diaconate. (*AG*, 15, 16)

There are so many faithful Catholic laymen actively teaching, preaching, presiding over scattered Christian communities, and practicing charity who could be strengthened by the imposition of hands, bound more closely to the altar, such that they could carry out their ministry more fruitfully via the sacrament of the diaconate. There are, indeed, some men who, while teaching in seminaries and Catholic colleges have requested and received ordination (after appropriate formation beyond their academic training). There are directors of religious education and youth ministers who have come forward, and, humbly entered into deacon formation, seeking that additional grace that would make their work in the vineyard of the Lord all the more fruitful.

Ad Gentes is that document of the Council that is oriented towards the missions:

> ... "Missions" is the term usually given to those particular undertakings by which the heralds of the Gospel, sent out by the Church and going forth into the whole world, carry out the task of preaching the Gospel and planting the Church among peoples or groups who do not yet believe in Christ. (*AG*, 6)

While we may not think of Western countries as missionary territory, the ongoing secularization of the West has been transforming Christendom into a "post-Christian" culture, at least from the perspective of the "secularizers." That is, countries such as France, Germany, the United States, and even Italy are becoming a new kind of mission territory. Is it possible that part of the reason for the restoration of the diaconate is this very trend? Did the Holy Spirit anticipate this need, inspiring the bishops at the Council?

- You men who are catechists, not only in the parishes, but also as professors in Catholic colleges and seminaries, as instructors in lay formation and catechesis programs: is the Spirit calling you through the Church to ordination, so that the Spirit will more effectively teach through you?

- You men who are working in Catholic charities and hospitals and evangelization projects, are you being called to strengthen your ministry and transform your identity?
- You businessmen who work hard to integrate Catholic ideals into the practicalities of the products you market and the services you offer, is the Spirit calling you to proclaim the Word, serve at the altar, and minister to your customers and employees in the power of the Spirit?
- You husbands and fathers, are you being called to strengthen the fulfillment of your responsibilities to your wife and children and witness the transforming power of Christ to the families of your children's friends and schoolmates, especially the children of separation and divorce?
- You medical men – physicians, dentists, optometrists, aides – as you seek to provide better health for your patients, are you being called by the Spirit to take the ministry of Word and altar into the practice of healing through the Spirit's power?
- You working men – heavy equipment operators, salesmen, truck drivers, firemen, police – are your love of God and your willingness to study the faith calling you to serve your bosses, fellow workers, and neighbors in the threefold ministry?

Deacon formation is not a walk in the park; its underlying dynamic is discernment. In addition to the intellectual challenge of acquiring and demonstrating a firm grasp of the Catholic Christian faith, the man must also progressively demonstrate appropriate receptivity to the Spirit, growth in love of God and neighbor, collaboration with fellow candidates, liturgical competence (service at the altar), and a diaconal ministerial orientation. Each of these "musts" is accompanied by continuous discernment, by both the man and his formators. Few men enter formation fully prepared in all of the dimensions of formation; they must study, practice, pray, and collaborate; they are to both follow and lead, especially demonstrating obedience. Obedience is more than "following orders"; rather it means listening, understanding, clarifying, and completing. In terms of the Catholic faith, the deacon is not only to accept all that the Church teaches; he is to understand the faith to the extent his own faculties permit and to be able to demonstrate that understanding in both word and action. As the ordaining Bishop admonishes:

Receive the Gospel of Christ

Believe what you read

Teach what you believe

Practice what you teach

You have read this book. Pray about it. Ask yourself what God is calling you to do. Married: ask your wife. Run it by your children. Query your pastor.

Whatever you decide let the Lord lead you:

Go and announce the Gospel of the Lord.

Go in peace, and glorify God by your life.

Go in peace.

References

The easiest way to locate these documents online is to search for them by full or partial title rather than the long web link, as often links are modified.

Basic Norms for the Formation of Permanent Deacons & Directory for the Ministry and Life of Permanent Deacons, 1998, Congregation for Catholic Education and Congregation for the Clergy, Libreria Editrice Vaticana, Vatican City, http://www. vatican. va/roman_curia/ congregations/ccatheduc/documents/rc_con_ccatheduc_doc_31031998_directo rium-diaconi_en. html

Benedict XVI, 2005, *Deus Caritas Est*, Encylical Letter, http://www.vatican.va/holy_father/benedict_xvi/encyclicals/documents/hf_ben-xvi_enc_20051225_deus-caritas-est_en.html

Benedict XVI, 2007, Sacramentum Caritatis, Post-Synodal Apostolic Exhortation on the Eucharist as the source and summit of the Church's life and mission,, February 22, http://www.vatican.va/holy_father/benedict_xvi/apost_exhortations/documents /hf_ben-xvi_exh_20070222_sacramentum-caritatis_en.html

Benedict XVI, 2007, Chrism Mass Homily, April 4, http://www.vatican.va/holy_father/benedict_xvi/homilies/2007/documents/hf_ ben-xvi_hom_20070405_messa-crismale_en.html

Benedict XVI, 2008, Address of His Holiness to the Bishops of the United States, April 16, http://www.vatican.va/holy_father/benedict_xvi/speeches/2008/april/document s/hf_ben-xvi_spe_20080416_bishops-usa_en.html,

Benedict XVI, 2010, General Audience, Saint Peter's Square Wednesday, April 14, http://www.vatican.va/holy_father/benedict_xvi/audiences/2010/documents/hf _ben-xvi_aud_20100414_en.html.

Clement of Rome to the Corinthians, c, 40-140 AD, http://www.earlychristianwritings.com/text/1clement-roberts.html

Congregation for Divine Worship and the Discipline of the Sacrament, 2004, *Redemptionis Sacramentum*, On certain matters to be observed or to be avoided regarding the Most Holy Eucharist, http://www. vatican. va/roman_curia/congregations/ccdds/ documents/rc_con_ccdds_doc_20040423_redemptionis-sacramentum_en. html

Congregation for the Doctrine of the Faith, Declaration *Inter Insigniores* on the question of the Admission of Women to the Ministerial Priesthood (October 15, 1976)

CWNews: Benedict XVI, April 5, 2007, "At Chrism Mass, Pope reflects on priest's vestments" http://www. cwnews. com/ news/viewstory. cfm?recnum=50344

John Paul II, 1980, *Dominicae Cenae*, Apostolic Exhortation, http://www. vatican. va/holy_father/john_paul_ii/letters/ documents/hf_jp-ii_let_24021980_dominicae-cenae_en. html

John Paul II, 1986, The Theology of marriage and Celibacy, St. Paul Editions

John Paul II, 1995, Letter to Women, June 29, http://www.vatican.va/holy_father/john_paul_ii/letters/documents/hf_jp-ii_let_29061995_women_en.html.

John Paul III, 1999, *Ordinatio Sacerdotalis*, Apostolic Letter On Reserving Priestly Ordination To Men Alone (http://www.ewtn.com/library/papaldoc/jp2ordin.htm)

Paul VI, 1967, *Sacerdotalis Caelibatus*, Encyclical, http://www. vatican. va/holy_father/paul_vi/encyclicals/documents/hf_p-vi_enc_24061967_sacerdotalis_en. html.

Paul VI, 1968, Pontificalis Romani recognition, Apostolic Constitution Approving New Rites of Ordination of Deacons, Priests, and Bishops, www.catholicliturgy.com/texts/pontrecognitio.txt.

Paul VI, 1975, Ordinatio Sacerdotalis, Apostolic Letter, On reserving priestly ordination to men alone, http://www.vatican.va/holy_father/john_paul_ii/apost_letters/1994/documents/hf_jp-ii_apl_19940522_ordinatio-sacerdotalis_en.html.

Paul VI, 1975, Response to the Letter of His Grace the Most Reverend Dr. F. D. Coggan, Archbishop of Canterbury, concerning the Ordination of Women to the Priesthood, November 30.

Pius XII, 1947, *Mediator Dei*, Encyclical http://www. vatican. va/holy_father/pius_xii/encyclicals/documents/hf_p-xii_enc_20111947_mediator-dei_en. html. .

Missale Romanum, General Instruction, Third Typical Edition, English Edition © 2010, International Commission on English in the Liturgy Corporation. (http://www. usccb. org/prayer-and-worship/the-mass/general-instruction-of-the-roman-missal/index. cfm)

Roberts, A. R., and Donaldson, J., editors, 1899, Constitution of the Apostles, Ante-Nicene Fathers, v. VII, Translations of the Fathers down to AD 325, American Edition, Eerdmans, Grand Rapids, MI. http://www. sacred-texts. com/chr/ecf/007/index. htm

Appendix: 1983 Code of Canon Law – canons relevant to permanent deacons

Canons included below do not form an exhaustive list; rather, those selected relate to the call to the vocation and its formation, the relationship of the diaconate to marriage, and the rights and responsibilities of the deacon. (**Emphasis** *is added.*)

Can. 89 A pastor and other presbyters or **deacons** are not able to dispense from universal and particular law unless this power has been expressly granted to them.

Can. 236 According to the prescripts of the conference of bishops, those aspiring to the **permanent diaconate** are to be formed to nourish a spiritual life and instructed to fulfill correctly the duties proper to that order... 2º men of a more mature age, whether **celibate** or **married**, are to spend three years in a program defined by the conference of bishops.

Can. 266 §1. Through the reception of the **diaconate**, a person becomes a cleric and is incardinated in the particular church or personal prelature for whose service he has been advanced.

Can. 276 §1. In leading their lives, clerics are bound in a special way to pursue holiness since, having been consecrated to God by a new title in the reception of orders, they are dispensers of the mysteries of God in the service of His people. ... §2. In order to be able to pursue this perfection: 1º they are first of all to fulfill faithfully and tirelessly the duties of the pastoral ministry; 2º they are to nourish their spiritual life from the two-fold table of sacred scripture and the Eucharist; therefore, priests are earnestly invited to offer the eucharistic sacrifice daily and **deacons** to participate in its offering daily; 3º priests and deacons aspiring to the presbyterate are obliged to carry out the liturgy of the hours daily according to the proper and approved liturgical books; **permanent deacons**, however, are to carry out the same to the extent defined by the conference of bishops; 4º they are equally bound to make time for spiritual retreats according to the prescripts of particular law; 5º they are urged to engage in mental prayer regularly, to approach the sacrament of penance frequently, to honor the Virgin Mother of God with particular veneration, and to use other common and particular means of sanctification.

Can. 281 §1. Since clerics dedicate themselves to ecclesiastical ministry, they deserve remuneration which is consistent with their condition, taking into account the nature of their function and the conditions of places and times, and by which they can provide for the necessities of their life as well as for the equitable payment of those whose services they need. ... §2. Provision must also be made so that they possess that social assistance which provides for their needs suitably if they suffer from illness, incapacity, or old age. §3. **Married**

deacons who devote themselves completely to ecclesiastical ministry deserve remuneration by which they are able to provide for the support of themselves and their families. Those who receive remuneration by reason of a civil profession which they exercise or have exercised, however, are to take care of the needs of themselves and their families from the income derived from it.

Can. 284 **Clerics** are to wear suitable ecclesiastical garb according to the norms issued by the conference of bishops and according to legitimate local customs. [cf. Can 288]

Can. 285 §1. **Clerics** are to refrain completely from all those things which are unbecoming to their state, according to the prescripts of particular law. ... §2. **Clerics** are to avoid those things which, although not unbecoming, are nevertheless foreign to the clerical state. §3. **Clerics** are forbidden to assume public offices which entail a participation in the exercise of civil power. §4. Without the permission of their ordinary, they are not to take on the management of goods belonging to lay persons or secular offices which entail an obligation of rendering accounts. They are prohibited from giving surety even with their own goods without consultation with their proper ordinary. They also are to refrain from signing promissory notes, namely, those through which they assume an obligation to make payment on demand. [cf. Can 288]

Can. 286 **Clerics** are prohibited from conducting business or trade personally or through others, for their own advantage or that of others, except with the permission of legitimate ecclesiastical authority. [cf. Can 288]

Can. 287 §1. Most especially, **clerics** are always to foster the peace and harmony based on justice which are to be observed among people. §2. They are not to have an active part in political parties and in governing labor unions unless, in the judgment of competent ecclesiastical authority, the protection of the rights of the Church or the promotion of the common good requires it. [cf. Can 288]

Can. 288 The prescripts of cann. 284, 285, §§3 and 4, 286, and 287, §2 do not bind **permanent deacons** unless particular law establishes otherwise.

Can. 290 Once validly received, sacred ordination never becomes invalid. A cleric, nevertheless, loses the clerical state: 1º by a judicial sentence or administrative decree, which declares the invalidity of sacred ordination; 2º by the penalty of dismissal lawfully imposed; 3º by rescript of the Apostolic See which grants it to **deacons** only for grave causes and to presbyters only for most grave causes.

Can. 517 §2. If, because of a lack of priests, the diocesan bishop has decided that participation in the exercise of the pastoral care of a parish is to be entrusted to a **deacon**, to another person who is not a priest, or to a community of persons, he is to appoint some priest who, provided with the powers and faculties of a pastor, is to direct the pastoral care.

Can. 519 The pastor (parochus) is the proper pastor (pastor) of the parish entrusted to him, exercising the pastoral care of the community committed to him under the authority of the diocesan bishop in whose ministry of Christ he has been called to share, so that for that same community he carries out the functions of teaching, sanctifying, and governing, also with the cooperation of other presbyters or **deacons** and with the assistance of lay members of the Christian faithful, according to the norm of law.

Can. 757 It is proper for presbyters, who are co-workers of the bishops, to proclaim the gospel of God; this duty binds especially pastors and others to whom the care of souls is entrusted with respect to the people committed to them. It is also for **deacons** to serve the people of God in the ministry of the word in communion with the bishop and his presbyterium.

Can. 764 Without prejudice to the prescript of can. 765, presbyters and **deacons** possess the faculty of preaching everywhere; this faculty is to be exercised with at least the presumed consent of the rector of the church, unless the competent ordinary has restricted or taken away the faculty or particular law requires express permission.

Can. 765 Preaching to religious in their churches or oratories requires the permission of the superior competent according to the norm of the constitutions.

Can. 767 §1. Among the forms of preaching, the homily, which is part of the liturgy itself and is reserved to a priest or **deacon**, is preeminent; in the homily the mysteries of faith and the norms of Christian life are to be explained from the sacred text during the course of the liturgical year. §2. A homily must be given at all Masses on Sundays and holy days of obligation which are celebrated with a congregation, and it cannot be omitted except for a grave cause. §3. It is strongly recommended that if there is a sufficient congregation, a homily is to be given even at Masses celebrated during the week, especially during the time of Advent and Lent or on the occasion of some feast day or a sorrowful event. §4. It is for the pastor or rector of a church to take care that these prescripts are observed conscientiously.

Can. 833 The following are obliged personally to make a profession of faith according to the formula approved by the Apostolic See: ... 6º in the presence of the local ordinary or his delegate and at the beginning of their function, pastors, the rector of a seminary, and teachers of theology and philosophy in seminaries; those to be promoted to the order of the **diaconate**;

Can. 835 §1. The bishops in the first place exercise the sanctifying function; they are the high priests, the principal dispensers of the mysteries of God, and the directors, promoters, and guardians of the entire liturgical life in the church entrusted to them. ... §2. Presbyters also exercise this function; sharing in the priesthood of Christ and as his ministers under the authority of the bishop, they are consecrated to celebrate divine worship and to sanctify the people. §3. **Deacons** have a part in the celebration of divine worship according to the norm of the prescripts of the law. §4. The other members of the Christian faithful also have their own part in the function of sanctifying by participating actively in their own way in liturgical celebrations, especially the Eucharist. Parents share in a particular way in this function by leading a conjugal life in a Christian spirit and by seeing to the Christian education of their children.

Can. 861 §1. The ordinary minister of baptism is a bishop, a presbyter, or a **deacon**, without prejudice to the prescript of can. 530, n. 1.

Can. 862 Except in a case of necessity, no one is permitted to confer baptism in the territory of another without the required permission, not even upon his own subjects.

Can. 907 In the eucharistic celebration **deacons** and lay persons are not permitted to offer prayers, especially the eucharistic prayer, or to perform actions which are proper to the celebrating priest.

Can. 910 §1. The ordinary minister of holy communion is a bishop, presbyter, or **deacon**.

Can. 929 In celebrating and administering the Eucharist, priests and **deacons** are to wear the sacred vestments prescribed by the rubrics.

Can. 930 §2. A blind or otherwise infirm priest licitly celebrates the eucharistic sacrifice by using any approved text of the Mass with the assistance, if needed, of another priest, **deacon**, or even a properly instructed lay person.

Can. 943 The minister of exposition of the Most Blessed Sacrament and of eucharistic benediction is a priest or **deacon**; ... the prescripts of the diocesan bishop are to be observed.

Can. 1008 By divine institution, the sacrament of orders establishes some among the Christian faithful as sacred ministers through an indelible character which marks them. They are consecrated and designated, each according to his grade so that they may serve the People of God by a new and specific title.

Can. 1009 §1. The orders are the episcopate, the presbyterate, and the **diaconate**. §2. They are conferred by the imposition of hands and the consecratory prayer which the liturgical books prescribe for the individual grades.

§3. Those who are constituted in the order of the episcopate or the presbyterate receive the mission and capacity to act in the person of Christ the Head, whereas **deacons** are empowered to serve the People of God in the ministries of the liturgy, the word, and charity.

Can. 1015 §1. Each person is to be ordained to the presbyterate or the **diaconate** by his proper bishop or with legitimate dimissorial letters from him. [*Note:*

Properly the name "dimissorial letters" refers to those given by a bishop or regular prelate to his subjects in order that they may be ordained by another bishop. Fanning, W. (1908). Dimissorial Letters. In The Catholic Encyclopedia. New York: Robert Appleton Company. Retrieved July 7, 2014 from New Advent: www. newadvent. org/cathen/04797b. htm]Can. 1016 As regards the **diaconal** ordination of those who intend to be enrolled in the secular clergy, the proper bishop is the bishop of the diocese in which the candidate has a domicile or the bishop of the diocese to which the candidate is determined to devote himself.

Can. 1027 Those aspiring to the **diaconate** and presbyterate are to be formed by careful preparation, according to the norm of law.

Can. 1031 §2. A candidate for the **permanent diaconate** who is not **married** is not to be admitted to the **diaconate** until after completing at least the Twenty-fifth year of age; one who is **married**, not until after completing at least the thirty-fifth year of age and with the consent of his wife.

§3. The conference of bishops is free to establish norms which require an older age for the presbyterate and the **permanent diaconate**.

Can. 1032 ... §3. A person aspiring to the **permanent diaconate** is not to be promoted to this order unless he has completed the time of formation.

Can. 1034 §1. A person aspiring to the **diaconate** or presbyterate is not to be ordained unless he has first been enrolled among the candidates through the liturgical rite of admission by the authority mentioned in [can.] 1016 ...; his petition is previously to have been written in his own hand, signed, and accepted in writing by the same authority.

Can. 1035 §1. Before anyone is promoted to the **permanent** or transitional **diaconate**, he is required to have received the ministries of lector and acolyte and to have exercised them for a suitable period of time. ... §2. There is to be an interval of at least six months between the conferral of the ministry of acolyte and the diaconate.

Can. 1036 In order to be promoted to the order of **diaconate** or of presbyterate, the candidate is to present to his bishop or competent major superior a declaration written in his own hand and signed in which he attests that he will receive the sacred order of his own accord and freely and will devote himself perpetually to the ecclesiastical ministry and at the same time asks to be admitted to the order to be received.

Can. 1037 An **unmarried** candidate for the **permanent diaconate** [is] not to be admitted to the order of diaconate unless [he has] assumed the obligation of **celibacy** in the prescribed rite publicly before God and the Church or have made perpetual vows in a religious institute.

Can. 1040 Those affected by any impediment, whether perpetual, which is called an irregularity, or simple, are prevented from receiving **orders**. The only impediments incurred, however, are those contained in the following canons.

Can. 1041 The following are irregular for receiving **orders**: 1º a person who labors under some form of amentia or other psychic illness due to which, after experts have been consulted, he is judged unqualified to fulfill the ministry properly; 2º a person who has committed the delict of apostasy, heresy, or schism; 3º a person who has attempted **marriage**, even only civilly, while either impeded personally from entering **marriage** by a matrimonial bond, sacred orders, or a public perpetual vow of chastity, or with a woman bound by a valid **marriage** or restricted by the same type of vow; 4º a person who has committed voluntary homicide or procured a completed abortion and all those who positively cooperated in either; 5º a person who has mutilated himself or another gravely and maliciously or who has attempted suicide; 6º a person who has placed an act of orders reserved to those in the order of episcopate or presbyterate while either lacking that order or prohibited from its exercise by some declared or imposed canonical penalty. [*Note:* Delict: a crime in canon law, an external violation of a law or precept gravely imputable by reason of malice or negligence. Glossary of Terms, www. vatican. va/resources/resources_glossary-terms_en. html, retrieved July 7, 2014]]

Can. 1042 The following are simply impeded from receiving orders: 1º a man who has a wife, unless he is legitimately destined to the **permanent diaconate**; 2º a person who exercises an office or administration forbidden to clerics according to the norm of cann. 285 and 286 for which he must render an account, until he becomes free by having relinquished the office or administration and rendered the account; 3º a neophyte unless he has been proven sufficiently in the judgment of the ordinary.

Can. 1043 If the Christian faithful are aware of impediments to sacred **orders**, they are obliged to reveal them to the ordinary or pastor before the ordination.

Can. 1044 §1. The following are irregular for the exercise of **orders** received: 1º a person who has received orders illegitimately while affected by an irregularity to receive them; 2º a person who has committed a delict mentioned in can. 1041, n. 2, if the delict is public; 3º a person who has committed a delict mentioned in can. 1041, nn. 3, 4, 5, 6. §2. The following are impeded from the exercise of orders: 1º a person who has received orders illegitimately while prevented by an impediment from receiving them; 2º a person who is affected by amentia or some other psychic illness mentioned in can. 1041, n. 1 until the ordinary, after consulting an expert, permits the exercise of the order. [*note:* Delict: See note with Can. 1041]

Can. 1045 Ignorance of the irregularities and impediments does not exempt from them.

Can. 1046 Irregularities and impediments are multiplied if they arise from different causes. They are not multiplied, however, if they arise from the repetition of the same cause unless it is a question of the irregularity for voluntary homicide or for having procured a completed abortion.

Can. 1047 §1. Dispensation from all irregularities is reserved to the Apostolic See alone if the fact on which they are based has been brought to the judicial forum. ... §2. Dispensation from the following irregularities and impediments to receive orders is also reserved to the Apostolic See: 1º irregularities from the public delicts mentioned in can. 1041, nn. 2 and 3; 2º the irregularity from the delict mentioned in can. 1041, n. 4, whether public or occult; 3º the impediment mentioned in can. 1042, n. 1. §3. Dispensation in public cases from the irregularities from exercising an order received mentioned in can. 1041, n. 3, and even in occult cases from the irregularities mentioned in can. 1041, n. 4 is also reserved to the Apostolic See. §4. An ordinary is able to dispense from irregularities and impediments not reserved to the Holy See. [*note:* Delict: See note with Can. 1041]

Can. 1048 In more urgent occult cases, if the ordinary or, when it concerns the irregularities mentioned in can. 1041, nn. 3 and 4, the Penitentiary cannot be approached and if there is imminent danger of grave harm or infamy, a person impeded by an irregularity from exercising an order can exercise it, but without prejudice to the obligation which remains of making recourse as soon as possible to the ordinary or the Penitentiary, omitting the name and through a confessor.

Can. 1049 §1. Petitions to obtain a dispensation from irregularities or impediments must indicate all the irregularities and impediments. Nevertheless, a general dispensation is valid even for those omitted in good faith, except for the irregularities mentioned in can. 1041, n. 4, and for others brought to the judicial forum, but not for those omitted in bad faith. §2. If it is a question of the irregularity from voluntary homicide or a procured abortion, the number of the delicts also must be mentioned for the validity of the dispensation. §3. A general dispensation from irregularities and impediments to receive orders is valid for all the orders. [*note:* Delict: See note with Can. 1041]

Can. 1050 For a person to be promoted to sacred orders, the following documents are required: 1º a testimonial that studies have been properly completed according to the norm of can. 1032; ... 3º for candidates to the **diaconate**, a testimonial that baptism, confirmation and the ministries mentioned in can. 1035 were received; likewise, a testimonial that the declaration mentioned in can. 1036 was made, and if the one to be ordained to the **permanent diaconate** is a **married** candidate, testimonials that the **marriage** was celebrated and the wife consents.

Can. 1055 §1. The matrimonial covenant, by which a man and a woman establish between themselves a partnership of the whole of life and which is ordered by its nature to the good of the spouses and the procreation and education of offspring, has been raised by Christ the Lord to the dignity of a sacrament between the baptized. §2. For this reason, a valid matrimonial contract cannot exist between the baptized without it being by that fact a sacrament.

Can. 1056 The essential properties of **marriage** are unity and indissolubility, which in Christian **marriage** obtain a special firmness by reason of the sacrament.

Can. 1057 §1. The consent of the parties, legitimately manifested between persons qualified by law, makes **marriage**; no human power is able to supply this consent. ... §2. Matrimonial consent is an act of the will by which a man and a woman mutually give and accept each other through an irrevocable covenant in order to establish **marriage**.

Can. 1079 §1. In urgent danger of death, the local ordinary can dispense his own subjects residing anywhere and all actually present in his territory both from the form to be observed in the celebration of **marriage** and from each and every impediment of ecclesiastical law, whether public or occult, except the impediment arising from the sacred order of presbyterate. §2. In the same circumstances mentioned in §1, but only for cases in which the local ordinary cannot be reached, the pastor, the properly delegated sacred minister, and the priest or **deacon** who assists at **marriage** according to the norm of can. 1116, §2 possess the same power of dispensing. §3. In danger of death a confessor possesses the power of dispensing from occult impediments for the internal forum, whether within or outside the act of sacramental confession. §4. In the case mentioned in §2, the local ordinary is not considered accessible if he can be reached only through telegraph or telephone.

Can. 1081 The pastor or the priest or **deacon** mentioned in can. 1079, §2 is to notify the local ordinary immediately about a dispensation granted for the external forum; it is also to be noted in the **marriage** register.

Can. 1108 §1. Only those **marriages** are valid which are contracted before the local ordinary, pastor, or a priest or **deacon** delegated by either of them, who assist, and before two witnesses according to the rules expressed in the following canons and without prejudice to the exceptions mentioned in cann. 144, 1112, §1, 1116, and 1127, §§1-2. ... §2. The person who assists at a **marriage** is understood to be only that person who is present, asks for the manifestation of the consent of the contracting parties, and receives it in the name of the Church.

Can. 1111 §1. As long as they hold office validly, the local ordinary and the pastor can delegate to priests and **deacons** the faculty, even a general one, of assisting at **marriages** within the limits of their territory. §2. To be valid, the delegation of the faculty to assist at **marriages** must be given to specific persons expressly. If it concerns special delegation, it must be given for a specific marriage; if it concerns general delegation, it must be given in writing.

Can. 1169 §1. Those marked with the episcopal character and presbyters permitted by law or legitimate grant can perform consecrations and dedications validly. ... §2. Any presbyter can impart blessings except those reserved to the Roman Pontiff or bishops. §3. A **deacon** can impart only those blessings expressly permitted by law.

Made in the USA
Lexington, KY
03 January 2017